BREAKING
INTO
BANKING

BREAKING INTO BANKING

THE ESSENTIAL GUIDE TO A CAREER IN FINANCE

AFZAL HUSSEIN

WILEY

Registered Offices
John Wiley & Sons, Inc., 111 River Street, Hoboken, NJ 07030, USA
John Wiley & Sons Ltd, The Atrium, Southern Gate, Chichester, West Sussex, PO19 8SQ, UK

For details of our global editorial offices, customer services, and more information about Wiley products visit us at www.wiley.com.

Wiley also publishes its books in a variety of electronic formats and by print-on-demand. Some content that appears in standard print versions of this book may not be available in other formats.

Library of Congress Cataloging-in-Publication Data is Available:

ISBN 9781394305025 (Paperback)
ISBN 9781394305032 (ePub)
ISBN 9781394305049 (ePDF)

Cover Design: Paul McCarthy
Cover Image: © Getty Images | Pulse

Set in MinionPro 11/16pt by Straive, Chennai, India.
Printed and bound by CPI Group (UK) Ltd, Croydon, CR0 4YY

C9781394305025_150525

The manufacturer's authorized representative according to the EU General Product Safety Regulation is Wiley-VCH GmbH, Boschstr. 12, 69469 Weinheim, Germany, e-mail: Product_Safety@wiley.com.

For Mum, Katherine, Amalia, and Kaia

CONTENTS

Contents

CONTENTS

Contents

CONTENTS

PREFACE

Breaking into the world of finance and banking is challenging. With rigorous application processes, high expectations, and intense competition, it can feel overwhelming for even the most ambitious and capable candidates. I know this because I've been through it. I've worked hard to secure multiple spring weeks, internships, and ultimately a full-time role at Goldman Sachs. This book is my way of sharing what I've learned along the way to make your journey into this industry smoother, more strategic, and, ultimately, successful.

The world of finance and banking is one of the most competitive industries to break into. Every year, hundreds of thousands of students and graduates set their sights on spring weeks, internships, and graduate schemes at top-tier firms, only to find themselves struggling to navigate the process. While there's no shortage of generic advice online, *what's missing is a clear, practical, and comprehensive roadmap tailored to finance and banking careers.* This book was written to fill that gap, giving you the tools and insights you need to stand out and succeed.

This is the book that I wish existed when I was in university applying to investment banks and financial institutions for spring weeks and internships. It's for the driven and ambitious individuals who are serious about starting a career in finance and banking. Whether you're yet to go to university, a first-year undergraduate exploring your options, a student preparing for applications or in the midst of interviews, or a graduate looking to maximise your chances of landing an entry-level role in the industry, this book is written for you. My goal is to guide you through every step of the process, leaving no stone unturned. From understanding the industry and identifying the most suitable career for you, to acing your applications and interviews.

When writing this book, I consciously made the decision to avoid writing just another theoretical guide. As such, this book is a practical resource packed with actionable advice and proven strategies for you to learn and apply. Every chapter is built on my personal experiences and the lessons I've learned helping thousands of individuals over the years. From explaining the nuances of different divisions to preparing for assessment centres and interviews, I've tried to provide everything you would need to succeed.

This book includes an Introduction followed by Part I: The Industry and Part II: Breaking In.

The Introduction provides some context and background information on me and my journey from growing up in a council estate, raised alongside four siblings by a single parent on income support, to breaking into the industry by securing tons of spring weeks, internships, and, eventually, a full-time role at Goldman Sachs.

Part I: The Industry takes a deep dive into the industry. It explains the key divisions and sectors within the world of finance and banking careers, typical career progression routes, the potential earnings you can unlock, the pros and cons of embarking on a career in this world, alternative careers, exit opportunities, and more. You'll also learn about the clients, roles, and responsibilities within some of the most competitive and sought-after divisions, and the skills required to enter and excel in them.

Part II: Breaking In focuses on practicalities. From writing a standout CV and mastering the art of networking to preparing for interviews and assessment centres, you'll find everything you need to know about the recruitment process. You'll also discover tips for building commercial awareness, effectively building and nurturing connections with industry professionals, and making the most of your early career opportunities.

This book isn't just a guide. It's a toolkit. It's built to empower you to navigate one of the toughest industries in the world with confidence and clarity. Whether you're aiming for a spring week, internship, or graduate scheme, this book will give you the edge you need to stand out in a crowded field. By the time you turn the final page, my hope is that you'll feel equipped to take on the challenges ahead and inspired to pursue your goals with determination.

Good luck. You got this!

ACKNOWLEDGEMENTS

Writing this book has truly been a labour of love, and I wouldn't have been able to do it without the help and support of some incredible people along the way.

First off, I want to thank my wife, Katherine. Your constant support, encouragement, and belief in me mean the world and carry me forward. Thank you for your feedback and putting up with the late nights and me disappearing into my work for hours on end.

Thank you to my family and friends for your infinite positivity and for always rooting for me. I wouldn't be where I am today without such a strong circle of individuals to lean on.

To the students, graduates, and professionals I've taught, connected, interacted, and worked with over the years—whether you've seen my videos online or met me in person, your questions, struggles, personal journeys, and wins have been a constant source of motivation for me to keep pushing and sharing what I know. Thank you.

To my editors and publishing team at Wiley—thank you for your feedback, patience, and for taking a chance on me. You've helped me write a book that I'm proud of, and for that I'm incredibly grateful.

And lastly, thank YOU. By picking up this book, you've taken a step towards building your future in finance and banking, and I hope this becomes a resource you turn to time and time again.

This book is the result of not just my work, but the collective wisdom, support, and inspiration of many people. Thank you to everyone who's been part of this journey.

ABOUT THE AUTHOR

Afzal Hussein is a finance professional turned educator, widely recognised as a leading voice in the finance and banking career space. With over 12 million views on YouTube and a quarter of a million followers across social media platforms, Afzal has built a trusted brand dedicated to helping students and graduates break into the competitive world of high finance.

Afzal's journey into finance began with relentless determination and strategic preparation, securing multiple spring weeks, internships, and eventually landing a coveted role at Goldman Sachs. His firsthand experience navigating the challenging recruitment processes and breaking into a high-pressure, results-driven environment inspired him to give back and empower others to do the same.

Through his engaging and relatable content, Afzal has become a go-to resource for career advice, covering everything from CV writing and interview preparation to developing commercial awareness and understanding the nuances of the different areas within the world of finance and banking. His unique ability to simplify complex topics while offering actionable insights has resonated with a global audience, helping thousands secure spring weeks, internships, and full-time roles at top-tier firms.

Afzal is also the founder of Finance Fast Track Academy, an online university-like community that provides free, accessible resources to students and graduates looking to kickstart their careers in finance. The academy boasts a thriving community of over 1,000 members and has become a cornerstone of Afzal's mission to democratise access to career success in the industry.

INTRODUCTION: FROM COUNCIL ESTATE TO GOLDMAN SACHS

B efore you dive into this book, I wanted to share how I managed to somehow end up in the front office of one of the most prestigious financial institutions in the world, Goldman Sachs. It's an unconventional story that combines life experiences from my childhood and early years, but one that I hope will inspire you to persist with the drive, determination, and discipline to pursue your goals even if it feels like the odds are stacked against you.

From a young age, I always knew that I wanted to put on a suit and work in the city. I'm not sure why, but I associated it with success and wealth and decided that I wanted to be a businessman, though I never really knew what that meant or how I would go about becoming one. I also never had any real insights or connections into careers in the city since I didn't know anyone who wore a suit to work.

After all, I grew up in a North West London council estate (for anyone unfamiliar with the term, a council estate is a government-funded housing complex) where the only careers we were exposed to were the youth workers at the local youth clubs, our school teachers, the local librarians, those who worked at the local chippy, betting shops, and newsagents, and those working for Camden Council.

Growing up in a council estate meant being surrounded by young people who were heavily involved in gangs, violence, drug deals, and other crimes and antisocial behaviour. A lot of the young people I grew up around came from extremely disruptive and fragmented homes, were in and out of prison, and had been stabbed by or had stabbed another young person from a different council estate. Youth clubs existed to keep us off the streets and provide a safe space where any young person could participate in recreational activities such as playing PlayStation, pool, football, table tennis, cooking, gym, and more.

My siblings and I were raised by an extremely strong single parent, my mum. We didn't have much, but we had all that we needed. Most importantly, my mum instilled a sense of awareness and direction in us during our formative years. This allowed us to attend the youth clubs and grow up with a lot of freedom and trust, but at the same time understand and appreciate the negative consequences of getting involved in gangs, trying or selling drugs, and mixing with the wrong people. Even so, the youth club was like a second home for us. We went to all the events, activities, trips, and tournaments. We were on good terms with all the young people, irrespective of what they were involved in outside of the youth club. Being particularly good at football, table tennis, and pool helped. But we made sure to keep our distance when it came to doing anything illegal or with potential negative consequences to our lives. Last but not least, we were surrounded by an amazing group of youth workers who always kept an eye out for us and made sure we stayed out of trouble.

From a career perspective, all we knew was that we had to perform well in school and college or sixth form in order to get into a good university, which would then open up a universe of career opportunities for us. And so that's what I did. I was a fairly mischievous kid, but I also got good grades throughout my school years.

After receiving my GCSE results, which were above average but not prodigy-esque, I had an important decision to make. I could stay at my school's sixth form and do International Baccalaureate (IB) or leave and go to a college and take my A-levels. I decided to go with the latter, and this is where, for the first time in my academic career, everything went downhill.

FAILURE: THE WAKE-UP CALL I NEEDED

In essence, the jump from GCSEs to A-levels caught me off guard. On top of this, I was attending a new college with a lack of focus or direction, and any real sense of why I was there. I knew a few people at the college but I felt like a lone ranger doing my own thing, and I was rudderless. Unfortunately for me, there were no spaces left in Economics which was the one subject I really wanted to learn about. So, I enrolled in AS Maths, Biology, Physics, and Geography. The lack of focus, guidance, and drive meant my mid-term grades suffered. For the first time, I was taking a massive academic hit. And for a few months, I didn't really care.

At the end of the first year I sat my AS exams and, a few months later, received my results. I 'achieved' a D in Maths, an E in Biology, a U in Physics, and a U in Geography. Grades I had never seen before. These results spoke for themselves and were the truest reflection of what happens when you fail to apply yourself. I honestly thought my life was over. I didn't know how I would go home and tell the news to my siblings, let alone my mum. So, I went home that day and caught my mum alone. I told her my results. I felt like a complete failure, and I knew I was better than this. To my surprise, she told me that it wasn't the end of the world, that I should leave the college and redo the year somewhere else. Such simple and straightforward advice. And it worked.

I used to be afraid of failing. I guess we're naturally taught that failure is bad, and succeeding is good. As time has gone on, and my view and perspective on life has matured, I can honestly say that I embrace the concept of failure. After all, every failure serves a purpose and offers a learning opportunity if you're open-minded enough to see it. My D, E, U, U results were the wake-up call I needed. I was comfortably complacent. This mega failure on my part was, to this day, one of the biggest blessings in disguise. Had I not failed so badly, only God knows what I'd be doing right now.

GETTING BACK ON TRACK

I knew something needed to change. I knew I was better than this. I knew I had to leave this college and find the drive and ambition that I always carried within me. So, I did what all younger siblings should do when they're in a time of need. I went to my eldest brother, who was very studious, and asked him for his advice.

He previously studied at Westminster City School's sixth form and only had good things to say about the place; he told me it was worth considering redoing my AS-levels there. I already had quite a few friends from football who were attending the school so I knew I'd fit in, and before I knew it, I had registered and secured my place.

Never did I think that I'd find myself retaking an academic year, but there I was, swallowing my pride and retaking a year with students a whole year younger than me. I felt like a total failure. When I got to Westminster City School, my game plan was simple. Do three AS-levels, not four, study like my life depended on it, go to class then go home and study, and avoid any and all distractions. At the end of the first year I received my grades, and wasn't surprised to find that I had achieved straight As in Maths, Economics, and Biology. I wasn't surprised because I had applied myself and remembered that performing well in exams is simply a combination of consistent effort and doing (and learning from) lots of past exam papers.

By the time I got into my second year, I had made more friends throughout the sixth form and was slightly 'less' focused on my studies compared to my first year. I was still studying hard and even won a scholarship, but I was also hanging around more often after the day was done, playing more football after hours with the guys, going out more, and generally spending more time in the common room instead of having my head in the books 100% of the time. Do I regret it? Not one bit. That sixth-form experience was amazing, and it allowed me to meet people who have become extremely close friends in my life today.

OFF TO UNIVERSITY

By the end of my final year at Westminster City School my grades got me into Queen Mary University of London (QMUL). QMUL wasn't my first choice, but in hindsight I wouldn't change studying there for the world. Not only because it's where I managed to secure spring weeks, internships, and meet lots of great people, but predominantly because it's where I met my wife. She helped me get into Goldman Sachs, and I helped her get into J.P. Morgan, but that's a story for another time…

During my time at university, I used to dream of securing a spring week because I knew how important it was to simply get my foot in the door. I knew that it would only get harder trying to break into the industry the longer I left it, or the less experience I had on my CV. I also knew that securing a spring week was easier than securing an internship, and securing an internship was easier than securing a graduate scheme. But the icing on the cake, for me, was finding out that you could convert a spring week into a summer internship, and you could convert a summer internship into a full-time role. Knowing all of this, I decided to be tactical and strategic regarding my approach to breaking into the industry, rather than follow the crowd and only apply for the toughest and fanciest roles out there.

FIRST YEAR: SPRING WEEKS

During my first year at university, I didn't really care which division I was breaking into because my mentality at the time was that beggars can't be choosers and, in my head, I was a beggar. My mentality was to secure anything, at any firm, and then build from there. After all, although QMUL was a great academic institution, and one of the Russell Group universities, it wasn't an elite institution like the London School of Economics, Oxbridge, or Harvard, and so I knew I needed an alternative way of standing out when it came to submitting my applications.

This led to a pretty straightforward plan. I knew that experience was the most in-demand 'currency', as opposed to having the best grades or going to an elite academic institution, so when it came to applications, I focused on securing as many experiences (irrespective of whether they were fancy front-office or less exciting back-office divisions) to (1) secure and convert a spring week into a summer internship in order to create a safety net and (2) enable me to apply to summer internships in my second year of university that were a little more risky (i.e. allow me to apply for front-office roles that I was actually interested in, with a solid CV full of broad finance experience). In simple terms, I just wanted to get my foot in the door.

During my first week of university, during induction week, I attended the compulsory sessions and introductions, and then immediately went home to apply for spring weeks. I met another guy who was doing the same thing and we clicked. We worked through applications, failed tests, improved our CVs and cover letters, and tried anything and everything to get invited to interviews and secure offers. Every other week we attended an insight evening at the Canary Wharf or other square-mile offices of bulge bracket investment banks. We also went to panel sessions and talks hosted by university finance and economics societies, and dreamed of being at the front of the room on the panel one day. As time went on, we formed a nice group of friends at QMUL who were all keen on breaking into the industry. We all helped each other and celebrated each other's wins. Some of us secured offers at investment banks, others ended up with consulting offers, but overall, we helped each other succeed which was nice. A large part of anyone's success comes from who they surround themselves with. So, I'd encourage you to constantly think about the people you have around you, in all areas of your life, not just career, because having the right people around you can save you a lot of time, stress, and effort.

BLACKROCK: MY INTRODUCTION TO ASSET MANAGEMENT

Before everyone jumped on the hype of applying to spring weeks, I was lucky enough to be proactive and secure some solid opportunities. One of these was a week's experience at BlackRock, the world's largest asset manager. This opportunity initially came about as a mentoring programme that was offered at QMUL, and to my surprise nobody seemed interested. Most people just hear and know about the sales and trading, or investment banking businesses, however, the industry is huge and has so much more on offer. I applied, secured a spot, and was mentored by an associate at BlackRock who was working in Fixed Income Portfolio Management. It was great, but the role was too technical for my interests, and since my strengths and interests were in public speaking, communication, and client-facing roles, I wanted to learn more about the sales roles available in the world of asset management. So, I reached out to the programme manager and asked them if they would be open to offering us mentees an informal insight week at BlackRock so we could explore the different career paths and roles that were on offer. It was well received, and we ended up with work experience (mostly shadowing) at BlackRock. This was a solid win for my CV and it opened my eyes to the world of asset management and the different career paths within.

EDF TRADING: A COLD EMAIL TO THE CEO'S ASSISTANT

Remember that scholarship I mentioned earlier? Well, since it was a scholarship in partnership with my old sixth form and the CEO of EDF Trading, I decided to email the CEO's assistant with a request for a potential internship or work experience on the firm's trading floor. A younger version of me would never have been so bold, but I was a young man on a mission. I told myself to always shoot my shot and always think about how insignificant the worst possible situation actually is. In this case, the worst possible situation would have been either being ignored or rejected. So, I sent the email and waited. Fortunately, it was great news. My proposal was considered and accepted. As a result, the other three scholars and I interned at EDF Trading during the summer of our first year of university. This was another strong experience to add to my CV.

ROYAL BANK OF SCOTLAND (NATWEST): OPERATIONS SPRING WEEK

During my first year of university, I did a few front-office applications, but prioritised back-office roles as my focus was purely on getting a foot into the industry through securing a spring week and then converting it into a summer internship offer the following year. One of these offers was an Operations Spring Week at the Royal Bank of Scotland (RBS), better known nowadays as NatWest. I remember skipping a university midterm exam to interview with RBS. Fortunately, it paid off. The spring week itself was a pleasant experience where I shadowed operations employees and got to meet and interact with interns from other divisions. My key takeaway from this spring week was the realisation that operations was most definitely not a career that I wanted to pursue. I wanted to be client-facing.

However, I still focused on acing the final day's interviews to try and convert the spring week into a summer internship for the following year. Fortunately, I was successful. Even though I knew I didn't want to work in operations, I was over the moon because I had been able to secure a 'safety-net' summer internship for the following year. This would allow me to double down on asset management internship applications in my second year of university. To my surprise, my plan was taking shape and working.

PRICEWATERHOUSE-COOPERS (PWC): CONSULTING, ACTUARIAL, TAX, OR ASSURANCE?

Lastly, I secured a place at PwC's Insight Academy, where they took us up to Leeds for half a week. It was less of a formal work experience where you shadow employees and do desk work, but more of a three-day assessment centre with lots of nice dinners with partners and activities and team-building exercises. It was great fun. At the end of the Insight Academy, we had the option of choosing which business area we were most interested in securing a place for the summer internship the following year.

The options were Consulting, Actuarial, Tax, and Assurance (Accounting). Everyone knew Consulting and Actuarial were the most competitive to break into (we were told by the staff that these business units had the least available headcount compared to the others), and so there I was, thinking tactically once again. I cared more about maximising my chances of securing an offer, as opposed to being picky about which offer I could secure. Personally, Tax sounded extremely boring, so I opted for the alternative option and went for Assurance. I had an interview, spoke about what I had learned throughout the academy, aced a few competency interview questions, and, to my luck, managed to impress enough to secure a place on the PwC Assurance Summer Internship the following year. I was over the moon.

FOUR FOR THE PRICE OF ONE

Whilst most students were trying to secure one spring week in extremely competitive areas such as investment banking or trading, I was more focused on securing many across a range of divisions and industries. And so, in my first year of university, I secured four experiences across asset management, trading, operations, and accounting. It honestly felt amazing going into my second year knowing that my CV was packed with a variety of finance-related experiences. On top of these experiences, I had also taken on quite a few extracurricular activities and leadership positions at university, as well as making the most of all the events that Sponsors for Educational Opportunity (SEO) London (a social mobility charity) hosted. As a result, I was feeling pretty confident about my chances of breaking into client-facing roles in asset management and private banking/private wealth management the following year. I told myself the best-case scenario would be breaking into asset management, and the worst-case scenario would be doing an assurance internship at PwC or an operations internship at RBS where I'd still be able to convert either of them into a full-time role.

With each experience I was fortunate enough to meet tons of like-minded people on a similar journey to me. This was actually extremely useful as it meant I was building and nurturing my network from a very early stage. The industry is a lot smaller than you might imagine, and as time goes on you never know how such connections and networks might evolve. This is why I encourage students and graduates to start building their networks, taking events seriously, and not just focusing on industry professionals from the get-go.

SECOND YEAR: INTERNSHIPS

When second year rolled around, my CV was looking great and I had one focus. Instead of only applying to back-office roles like I did in the first year, I would only apply to front-office roles for internships (specifically, asset management and private banking/private wealth management). Why? Well, firstly, I already had internship offers secured for operations at RBS and assurance at PwC. And, secondly, having spent time at BlackRock, I knew I wanted to work in the world of investment management given the alignment of my core strengths and career interests. Investment banking didn't attract me one bit due to the long hours and lifestyle, nor did the early mornings, markets focus, and intensity of the trading floor.

After tons of applications, online tests, versions of my CV and cover letter, assessment centres, interviews, and rejections, I managed to secure an offer from none other than Goldman Sachs within their Asset Management business. The prospect of securing a summer internship at Goldman Sachs wasn't only out of my expectations, it was beyond my wildest dreams. It makes me laugh because I submitted my application the day before the deadline, and I missed the initial phone call when the HR team wanted to notify me of having successfully secured a place on the programme. I emailed them immediately, they called me back, and being told I had secured an offer at Goldman Sachs Asset Management was one of the greatest feelings of my academic career. I tried not to get carried away, however, as I was eagerly waiting for the contract to arrive so I could sign it and get everything set in stone before celebrating or even mentioning the exciting news to anyone outside of my family.

True story, I almost went with Barclays for their Private Banking internship programme instead of Goldman Sachs. With all due respect, I thought I'd have a higher chance of converting the internship at Barclays into a full-time role. Luckily, I ignored my negative self-talk, consulted my close circle of family and friends, and went all in on Goldman Sachs.

I spent 10 weeks in the Consultant Relations team, which is the team in the world of asset management responsible for managing relationships with investment consultants, who are effectively the gatekeepers to a lot of client capital. Investment consultants rate the products we offer clients to invest in and they advise their clients (pension funds, insurance companies, etc.) whether to consider investing with the firm or not.

The internship included tons of catch-ups, presentations, networking and social events, desk work, client meetings (I had a great manager who gave me client exposure early on), group projects, late nights past midnight, expensed dinners, and a final presentation in front of everyone I met during the internship. After 10 intense weeks, I managed to head back to university knowing I gave it my all. There was nothing left to do, but wait for a phone call to either let me know that I had failed and wouldn't be receiving a full-time offer, or that I had succeeded and secured a spot to join full-time after my graduation.

A few weeks after the internship had ended, I was in Mile End, near QMUL, playing football when I checked my phone during a break. *1 missed call.* I can't exactly remember if I returned the call or if it automatically rang again, but it was my manager. I was extremely nervous before she told me the good news. She told me that the team really enjoyed having me over the summer and that they'd be delighted to offer me a full-time position after I had finished my final year at university and graduated. You know the feeling I described earlier when I secured the summer internship? This feeling topped that, tenfold. I was lost for words. It was a no-brainer for me. It was an immediate yes. I just needed to wait for the contract to arrive so I could sign it. The added bonus was that I knew I wouldn't have to submit a single graduate scheme application going forward because I had just secured the only full-time role that I was interested in, at the firm of my dreams. I felt blessed and truly grateful. My strategic approach to breaking into banking was working.

THIRD YEAR: TAKING A BREATHER

I went into my third year of university pretty chilled and relaxed, knowing that I had the best possible career offer already in the bag. Word went around and the general reaction was excitement and congratulations from my friends, and confusion from anyone that knew of me, but didn't know me. I say this without any intention of sounding arrogant, but it was rare for someone from my university, let alone someone growing up on free school meals, in a single-parent household on a council estate, to break into a front-office role at Goldman Sachs. But there I was. Somehow, I did it. I turned my focus to my studies (I honestly hated studying, found it completely pointless, and only went to university because it was needed to secure a spring week and internship), and tried to help as many of my friends with their CVs, cover letters, and applications as possible.

GRADUATING: GOLDMAN SACHS AND LIVING LARGE IN NEW YORK

After my final year of university was done and dusted, Goldman Sachs flew me and all of the new analysts out to New York for global training. In those six weeks I met the New York Consultant Relations team, networked as much as I could, and we had tons of structured learning, workshops, presentations, networking sessions, socials, and so much more. For many of us it was our first time in New York, so we used every opportunity to go out to explore the city, visit museums, watch Broadway shows, eat, shop, and explore. It was the summer that Germany won the World Cup, the weather was perfect, and I felt like I was living the good life. Once New York training was over we all flew back home and started as full-time analysts a few weeks later, in September. And that's the story of how I broke into the industry. The rest is history.

PART I

THE INDUSTRY

CHAPTER 1

THE INDUSTRY BEFORE AND AFTER THE 2008 GLOBAL FINANCIAL CRISIS

I n order to understand the world we live in today, we need to look back and understand the world of the past. In this chapter I'll explain some of the key differences across the world of finance and banking before and after the Global Financial Crisis (GFC) of 2008. In doing so, I hope to set the scene and manage your expectations for what the world of finance and banking has in store for you in the world of today, almost two decades on from the GFC.

The world of finance and banking is vastly different today than it was before 2008. Before 2008, careers in finance were marked by rapid growth, extremely competitive and lucrative compensation packages, and significant opportunities for advancement and career growth. The focus on short-term profits, combined with an industry that wasn't anywhere near as regulated as it is today, contributed to the vulnerabilities that would eventually lead to the collapse of the American housing market and subsequently the GFC.

Before 2008, the regulatory environment was relatively lenient, which led to excessive risk-taking and unsupervised financial innovation. As a result, we saw the creation of complex financial products and an increase in market liberalisation. After 2008, markets became increasingly stringent with the introduction of new regulations such as the Dodd–Frank Act and Basel III, both focused on increasing financial transparency, reducing financial risk, and protecting customers.

On the compensation front, before 2008, salaries, bonuses, and other financial incentives such as stock options were highly competitive, and heavily tied to short-term financial goals and performance. The lack of regulation meant excessive risk-taking was normal and the focus on high-risk, high-reward strategies resulted in millions of dollars' worth of earnings for top performers, especially those in revenue-generating roles such as trading and investment banking.

Since then, compensation structures have become more conservative, with a greater emphasis on long-term performance and deferred bonuses (i.e. firms paying bonuses in cash and stock whereby an employee is able to vest [unlock] their stock earnings contingent on them working for the firm for a few more years). Should they decide to quit or change careers, they would be giving up any unvested stock options. Additionally, benefits packages started focusing on employee well-being and stability by offering improved health insurance and retirement benefits.

One thing that hasn't changed much before and after 2008 are the long working hours that the industry has a notorious reputation for. The world of finance, or high finance, is known for overworking its junior professionals through 80–100-hour weeks. This, however, is mostly the case within the investment banking division. And as much as I'd like to tell you otherwise, this is unfortunately still the case today.

Back when I was interning at Goldman Sachs in 2013, an intern in the investment banking division of another global investment bank passed away after working for 72 hours straight. He was only 1 week away from completing his internship. In 2024, an associate in the investment banking division of the same firm also passed away; 100-hour working weeks were cited to have played a part. More than 10 years later and it's still happening.

Nowadays, however, there's a greater emphasis on the importance of work–life balance, particularly for junior professionals. But, in all honesty, and at the end of the day, if there's a ton of client work that needs to get done ahead of a given deadline, someone (usually the junior employees) still have to take care of it, or risk ruining their reputation to the team, whilst also potentially losing the firm the business, or even worse, the client.

This pressure on employees trickles down from the top. The shareholders put pressure on the board of directors. The board of directors put pressure on the C-suite executives. The partners are under pressure from the C-suite executives. And this pressure then trickles down onto the most junior employees who bear a huge brunt of the pressure and subsequent workload. Everyone wants to get the work done by any means necessary because they don't want to look bad or get fired, and when all is said and done, they hope to receive a bonus that's a multiple of their base salary. As such, it's not uncommon for the most junior employees, interns and analysts, to work from 8/9 am to way past midnight, implementing feedback on presentation slides and updating financial models (used to evaluate companies, transactions, and deals) ahead of upcoming client meetings and pitches.

Before 2008, the most commonly sought-after roles by graduates, partly because they paid the most and led to the most lucrative career opportunities, were on the trading floor or in advisory positions within the investment banking division. Since 2008, and since the move away from short-termism, a number of other revenue-generating roles have grown in popularity. These include investment and client relationship roles across asset/investment management, similar roles in private banking and wealth management, and investment research roles. Other areas that have gained prominence include risk management, compliance, and in most recent times, technology.

In terms of educational background and qualifications, the industry has always had a preference for hiring candidates from the most elite academic institutions all over the world. Qualifications like the Chartered Financial Analyst (CFA) and Master of Business Administration (MBA) were once highly attractive to employers and proved common pathways into top finance roles at the most prestigious institutions. This is still true today, however, to a lesser extent. Firms are recognising and embracing the benefits of hiring from diverse backgrounds, races, genders, and academic institutions, to name a few.

Furthermore, they're also realising the value of hiring graduates from a range of degree disciplines such as the sciences, technology, engineering, maths, social sciences, languages, and so on, as opposed to only focusing on hiring economics and finance graduates. Although I studied economics and finance, the analyst to my left when I was at Goldman Sachs studied Spanish at university, whilst the analyst behind me studied history.

Whilst we're on the topic of diversity, it's worth noting that the industry has always had room for improvement. And it has improved. Before 2008, it was rare to see women in numbers on the trading floor or any of the other revenue-generating divisions, let alone seeing them occupy senior positions and leading entire businesses. This isn't the case today (although there's still a lot of work that needs to be done).

Last but not least, the industry was only beginning to take advantage of the advancements in technology in 2008. Quantitative finance and quantitative trading were becoming prominent, driving innovation on the trading floor and across risk management divisions. However, this is minuscule in comparison to the growth in technological advancements made since then, and more so particularly now, given the recent adoption and growth of artificial intelligence and machine learning by major financial institutions and investment banks.

It's fair to say that the world of finance has undergone significant changes since the 2008 GFC. While the pre-crisis era was marked by substantial growth, high rewards, excessive risk-taking, and lenient regulation, the post-crisis era has prioritised the avoidance of repeating previous mistakes, a dedication to risk management, welcoming more stringent regulations, and a focus on sustainability and longevity.

CHAPTER 2

BULGE BRACKETS VERSUS BOUTIQUES

When we think about the types of firms within the industry, we can broadly split them into two main categories: bulge bracket firms, or more commonly 'bulge brackets', and boutique firms, or more commonly 'boutiques'. They differ in many ways, including work–life balance, the range of services they offer to their clients, the roles, responsibilities, and career progression routes available to employees, compensation packages, exit opportunities, and organisational culture, to name a few.

However, the biggest difference between bulge brackets and boutiques is size. Bulge brackets can employ anywhere from 5,000 to more than

200,000 people, whereas boutiques typically have between 200 and 5,000 employees. Firms with less than 20 employees are considered startups, whilst firms with 20–200 employees are often termed scale-ups.

When we talk about bulge brackets we're mostly referring to global investment banks such as Goldman Sachs, J.P. Morgan, Morgan Stanley, and so on. These firms are considered global because they service clients in offices all over the world. They also encompass a range of different divisions, including the Investment Banking Division, Sales and Trading, Asset Management, Private Wealth Management or Private Banking, Investment Research, Operations, Technology, Audit, Finance, Legal, Human Resources, Compliance, and more.

In contrast, boutiques are smaller, more specialised investment banks, asset managers, or trading firms. They still have the support functions and divisions enabling the front office to perform effectively, except these divisions will be a lot smaller compared to bulge brackets. Boutiques are simply too small to offer the depth and variety of services that bulge bracket investment banks typically offer. However, this is by choice. Boutiques are small and nimble. They specialise and focus their offering on specific sectors, services, clients, or regions. By being specialists, their competitive advantage offers an extremely specific service for an extremely specific client base. Many clients prefer this high-touch, personal service as opposed to being one of the hundreds of clients that bulge bracket banks serve.

With that, let's dive into the nuances that come with working for bulge brackets versus working for boutiques.

Roles and responsibilities are broadly similar at each level between the two types of firms. However, it's worth noting that you're likely to get more ownership and responsibility at a boutique over a bulge bracket. You can think of it in the following way: when you work for a large investment bank, you're like one tiny cog in a huge machine. Inside this machine there are tens of thousands of other moving pieces (your colleagues) and so it can be hard to stand out.

Contrast this with being a larger cog in a small machine. In this environment, you're more likely to get noticed, receive more responsibility, and be given more ownership of work to take a lead on. This is why progression at boutiques can often be faster than at bulge brackets, particularly because many boutiques have less of a formal hierarchical structure.

Salaries can vary across boutiques and bulge brackets, with the major influencing factors being the firms themselves and each individual role. Other impacting factors include current market conditions, firm performance, team performance, individual performance, regulations, and more. For example, if we were in a recession it's more likely that bonuses will be smaller versus if we were in a booming economy.

The culture at some boutiques tends to be less pressured and more relaxed compared to the culture at most bulge bracket firms. However, other boutiques will experience greater pressure since there's 'no room to hide' at a smaller firm.

If you're wondering which is better to start your career in, I would personally recommend pursuing a career at a bulge bracket firm first, before considering moving into a specialist boutique later on in your career. There are a few reasons for this.

Firstly, brand reputation is extremely important when it comes to unlocking new opportunities as a student, graduate, or professional. Working for a bulge bracket investment bank like Goldman Sachs or J.P. Morgan carries a lot of weight and brand reputation that will get you noticed more than working at a 'lesser' known boutique would.

Secondly, it's trickier to break into boutiques at the entry level as they typically don't have as many structured programmes like spring weeks or internships for students and graduates compared to bulge brackets. To add to this, given the nature and size of boutiques, they typically hire fewer people each year, especially at the junior levels, compared to bulge bracket firms. An internship class at Goldman Sachs can range from 2,000 to 4,000 interns globally, whereas an internship class at a boutique can be 5 to 10 interns.

Lastly, working for a bulge bracket firm offers an extensive level of exposure into the different businesses/divisions within an investment bank. This exposure is particularly useful early on in your career as you're still trying to figure out what part of the financial world you're most interested in and which specific career you want to pursue over the next 30 or 40 years. Most global investment banks would rather you move internally (i.e. from the investment banking division into the asset management business, or from the operations division into sales and trading), as opposed to having you leave the firm altogether.

There are two main advantages of working for a boutique firm early on in your career. The first is that you'll likely be given more responsibility early on given that you're one of a handful of interns or analysts. If you're exceptional you'll likely be able to climb and get promoted a lot faster than you would at a bulge bracket. Bulge brackets typically have a formal hierarchical structure that makes sure every junior professional (analysts and associates) spends a certain number of years at that level before being promoted to the next rung of the ladder (unless the individual is truly exceptional and the firm isn't willing to risk losing them to a competitor). The more senior you become, the less defined the tenure requirements are in order to progress up the ladder.

The second advantage of working for a boutique early on in your career is that you'll be able to niche down and become a specialist in a specific industry and sector very fast—this is good if you already know which specific career you want to pursue within the world of finance. However, what typically happens after you enter the industry is that you get to learn what you're actually interested in and like doing, you discover and explore new and unexpected opportunities, and essentially pivot from there.

Popular boutique investment banks like Rothschild & Co., Evercore, and Lazard offer spring weeks, summer internships, and graduate programmes. However, this isn't the case for all boutiques. The general rule is that the more niche a boutique firm is (irrespective of whether it's focused on investment banking, asset management, sales and trading, research, consulting, etc.), the less likely it is to have a structured spring week or internship programme.

As a student or graduate, it's worth considering both bulge brackets and boutiques when applying for spring weeks, internships, and graduate schemes. If you don't have your dreams set on a particular niche or division, my advice would be to focus on getting a foot in the door as experience is all that really matters in the earlier part of your career journey.

For free resources on breaking into the industry visit www.afzalhussein.com.

CHAPTER 3

BUY SIDE VERSUS SELL SIDE

A lot of candidates know about the different divisions of investment banks and the various sectors across the world of finance and banking, but aren't too familiar with the concept of the buy side and the sell side. Knowing the difference between the buy side and the sell side is important and so in this chapter I'll cover it in as much detail as you'll need for interviews.

Essentially, the buy side is responsible for managing capital for its clients (and often the firm itself) by purchasing assets from the sell side. And the sell side is responsible for creating, issuing, and selling financial instruments and securities to the buy side. The sell side creates and sells financial products, whilst the buy side holds the capital and purchases these financial securities in order to meet investment objectives. Last but not least, buy-side firms mostly focus on generating revenue from investment returns, whilst the sell side focuses on generating revenue by charging a fee for executing transactions or offering advisory services.

Examples of companies on the buy side include asset managers and private wealth managers who are investing large sums of capital across asset classes on behalf of their institutional and high-net-worth clients, private equity firms who are investing their clients' capital across private businesses, venture capital firms who are investing their clients' capital into early-stage startups, and hedge funds who are investing aggressively across the financial markets on behalf of their clients, as well as for themselves. These firms all have capital at their disposal that needs to be deployed and invested. As a result, buy-side firms will interact with sell-side firms (investment banks, brokerage firms, and market-makers) in order to buy the financial products they're most interested in.

Examples of firms on the sell side include investment banks (excluding the asset management and private wealth management divisions), commercial banks, brokerage firms or stockbrokers, and market-makers (the sales and trading floor where they're connecting buyers and sellers to create a market, and taking a commission for their assistance).

This whole concept of buy side versus sell side can be quite confusing when it comes to bulge bracket investment banks in particular. After all, they're considered sell-side institutions because most of their revenue comes from sell-side activities like investment banking (advisory services and capital raising) and global markers or sales and trading (market-making). However, given that bulge bracket investment banks like to diversify their revenue streams by having multiple revenue-generating divisions, they end up participating in the buy side as well as the sell side. For example, the buy-side divisions within investment banks include the asset management and private wealth management businesses. Not to mention many investment banks also offer alternative investment opportunities and thus have products and teams working across the firm's own private equity, venture capital, and hedge fund teams, or mini-divisions.

On the other hand, we also have pure-play asset managers like Black-Rock, and firms like the Carlyle Group who focus solely on private equity, both of which are buy-side firms. Hedge funds, private equity, and venture capital firms are examples of companies strictly on the buy side. Meanwhile, pure-play or boutique investment banks like Lazard, Rothschild, and Evercore focus exclusively on mergers and acquisitions (M&As), capital raising, and underwriting activities, which are all on the sell side.

Understanding the key distinctions between the buy side and sell side will set you apart in interviews, especially if you're able to articulate why you're interested in a particular role or division and how it relates to your preference for working on the buy side or the sell side.

Although most front-office roles are split across these sides, it's worth noting that middle and back-office divisions will exist irrespective of the buy side or sell side. Why? Well, these divisions (risk management, human resources, operations, compliance, technology, legal, etc.) are all needed in order for firms to function. More specifically, they're needed in order for the front-office businesses to be able to carry out their roles efficiently, effectively, and legally without breaking any rules from a regulatory standpoint.

Let's talk about why each side exists and how they serve their respective clients. The sell side exists in order to serve clients who need access to capital, liquidity (the ability to turn financial securities or investments into cash), and advisory services. In contrast, the buy side exists in order to serve clients who already have capital, typically don't need (immediate) liquidity, and require assistance investing the capital that they have. The sell side aims to generate returns by selling securities on behalf of their clients, or taking fees for helping their clients raise capital. As opposed to the buy side, which aims to buy assets to generate investment returns, whilst also charging fees for doing so successfully.

In terms of work–life balance, generally speaking, sell-side roles tend to come with a more pressurised working environment, and have longer working hours due to client demands around the clock, while buy-side roles tend to offer relatively better work–life balance, and higher pay as you become more senior. This is why it's quite common for graduates to break into the investment banking division and use it as a training ground by spending two or three years mastering their financial model-building and valuation skills, before pivoting into private equity or a hedge fund where the compensation is typically higher, and although still not a nine to five, the work–life balance is better.

If you're wondering why graduates spend time breaking into investment banking before making the move to private equity, it's because there tend to be a lot more investment banking opportunities in the form of spring weeks, internships, and graduate schemes available. Although private equity and hedge fund opportunities do exist for students and graduates, they're extremely hard to come by or difficult to break into from the outset. As such, the more common route is to work for an investment bank for a few years before moving over.

CHAPTER 4

ASSET CLASSES

You're probably wondering what exactly these buy-side firms invest their clients' capital into and how does this concept of investing money into the financial markets work. After all, the terms 'financial markets' and 'investing' are quite broad. At its core, investors can deploy capital into different 'asset classes', which are like different 'flavours' or options available for investors to spend their money across.

Each asset class has its own unique characteristics that differentiate it from the others. Each investor will be in a unique situation which brings about their own unique goals and objectives for investing. They'll have different investment goals, preferences, time horizons, risk appetites, and so on that'll need to be considered before investing any of their capital. As such, asset classes provide the required characteristics that investors are most interested in. Some asset classes will offer a higher return but will require taking on substantial risk, whilst others will offer lower returns because they're lower-risk investments, or high potential returns if you're willing to tie up your money for a long period of time. There's lots of different factors that impact and influence a potential investment's returns, and these can be explored through the various asset classes on offer to investors.

There are seven main asset classes:

- Fixed income (debt)
- Equities (stocks)
- Commodities
- Currencies
- Alternatives
- Cash
- Real estate

Most investments will typically fall into one of these categories. It's worth noting that smaller buy-side firms may specialise in one or two specific asset classes, whilst larger asset managers have larger teams and resources for all asset classes.

FIXED INCOME (DEBT)

Fixed income refers to investments that provide a regular and fixed income (i.e. interest payments) plus the return of the principal amount at maturity (i.e. at the end of the contract). Fixed income simply means debt products where one party is borrowing money from another. Common examples of fixed-income products include government bonds, corporate bonds, and municipal bonds. These investments are generally considered lower risk compared to the alternatives or equities asset classes, and are often used for income generation and capital preservation. This asset class is often used in portfolios to provide stability and protection against market volatility.

EQUITIES (STOCKS)

Equities, otherwise known as stocks, represent ownership in a company or companies. When you invest in equities, you essentially become a shareholder of that company, with the potential to earn returns through price appreciation and dividends. Equities are a key growth component in investment portfolios as they offer higher potential returns than most fixed-income investments. Having said this, generally speaking, if an investment offers a high return, it usually comes with higher risk. Equities are split up by market capitalisation (small-cap, mid-cap, and large-cap), sectors (technology, healthcare, etc.), and geographic regions. They tend to be suitable for investors with a higher risk tolerance and a long-term investment horizon, as they can provide significant capital growth over time.

COMMODITIES

Commodities are tangible assets like gold, oil, natural gas, and agricultural products such as wheat and coffee. They're traded on commodities markets, and their prices are influenced by supply and demand, geopolitical events, and economic conditions. Commodities can act as a hedge (offer protection) against inflation, since their prices often rise when inflation increases. You can gain exposure to commodities through direct ownership, futures contracts, or commodity-focused funds. Whilst commodities can provide diversification benefits to an investment portfolio, they're also known for high volatility and are typically considered a more speculative asset class.

CURRENCIES (FOREIGN EXCHANGE)

The currency, or foreign exchange markets involve trading one currency against another in the global currency markets. The currency market is the largest and most liquid (ease of which you can trade an investment for cash) market in the world, operating 24 hours a day, 7 days a week. Like most asset classes, the foreign exchange market is influenced by a wide range of factors, including interest rates, economic data, geopolitical events, and market sentiment. Investors and institutions trade currencies for various reasons, including hedging against currency risk, speculation, and facilitating international trade. It's worth noting that currency investments can be volatile and are considered high risk, often attracting traders looking for short-term profit opportunities rather than long-term investors.

ALTERNATIVES

Alternative investments encompass a broad category of assets that fall outside traditional investments like stocks, bonds, and cash. This category includes private equity, hedge funds, venture capital, cryptocurrencies, and collectibles such as art. It can also include commodities and real estate; however, these are large enough to warrant being categorised as asset classes themselves. Alternatives often provide access to riskier investments in return for seeking higher returns and greater portfolio diversifications (they tend to have a low correlation with traditional asset classes). Oftentimes, the average person won't be able to invest in complex alternative vehicles such as hedge funds, which are only available to institutional and accredited investors. Lastly, alternatives, for the most part, tend to be more expensive to access, and offer less liquidity (ease of access to your capital) compared to the other asset classes.

CASH

Cash and cash equivalents include physical currency, savings accounts, money-market funds, and short-term government securities like Treasury bills. This asset class is extremely liquid and a safe space for investing money that you might need rapid access to. Cash assets are highly liquid, meaning they can be easily converted to cash without significant loss of value. Investors like investing in the cash asset class as it provides safety and stability, offering a place to park unused funds temporarily or as a reserve for emergencies. Having said this, cash does come with a downside. It typically earns lower returns than other asset classes, given its low-risk nature, and it can lose purchasing power over time due to the impact of inflation.

REAL ESTATE

Last but not least, real estate involves investing in physical properties such as residential homes, commercial buildings, and land. These investments are known for generating income through rent whilst also offering the potential for appreciation in value over time. Real-estate investors can also gain exposure to real estate through Real Estate Investment Trusts (REITs), which pool investor money to buy and manage properties. Real estate is often seen as a tangible, inflation-protected asset that can diversify a portfolio. Although it offers long-term growth potential, the asset class also comes with challenges like market fluctuations, property management, and liquidity issues, making it suitable for investors with longer investment horizons and a greater tolerance for risk.

CHAPTER 5

DIVISIONS

FRONT OFFICE

Every investment bank can be broken up into three parts: the front office, the middle office, and the back office. Each consists of a number of divisions which are at a similar hierarchical level within the structure of the firm. Though this may sound quite confusing, it's pretty straightforward to understand. For example, the front office is responsible for revenue generation. As such, the divisions that directly generate revenue for the firm are considered front-office divisions. Examples of these divisions include investment banking, asset management, sales and trading, private wealth management, and investment research.

These front-office divisions share a few characteristics, including the following: they generate revenue for the investment bank, they are client-facing divisions (i.e. they build and manage client relationships to bring in new business), they tend to pay higher base salaries and bonuses than the other (middle and back-office) divisions, and, last but not least, working in these divisions typically requires employees to work longer hours, and thus have poorer work–life balance, than employees working in middle and back-office roles.

In contrast, the middle-office divisions include risk management and treasury services, whilst the back office includes divisions such as human resources, operations, finance, legal, audit, technology, and compliance.

The main thing to understand here is that the front office is responsible for generating revenue for the firm, whilst the middle and back office are responsible for enabling the front office, and the rest of the firm, to operate as efficiently and effectively as possible.

The Nature of the Work

In the front office, work typically involves interacting with clients, making investment decisions, executing trades, carrying out market research, and providing financial advisory services. These responsibilities will vary from division to division. For example, if you're working on the trading floor you'll be responsible for things like executing trades for clients or providing your own in-depth market research and opinions on particular areas of the financial markets to clients. In contrast, if you're working in the investment banking division your responsibilities will include providing advice on how your clients could achieve their strategic goals, whether that be to raise capital through the debt or equity markets, acquire a competitor, or merge with an incumbent in the same industry. To add to that, if you're working in the asset management or private wealth management divisions then the nature of your work, together with your responsibilities, will centre around building and nurturing long-term client relationships (if you're in a sales-focused role) or investing over time to generate returns or protect capital for your clients (if you're in an investing role) with a focus on achieving your clients' long-term investment goals.

Therefore, working in the front office provides a range of opportunities and options to work in revenue-generating roles. It's also worth knowing that there are positions within these front-office divisions that are more client facing than others. For example, a salesperson on the trading floor will naturally have more client interaction and exposure compared to the trader who's analysing financial markets data on their screens for the majority of their day. Similarly, client interaction will be a larger part of the salesperson's role within the asset management or private wealth management businesses compared to the product specialists and portfolio managers within these divisions.

Contributions to the Company's Overall Success

The front office is the main revenue-generating part of an investment bank. It drives the firm's profitability through its various front-office divisions (investment banking, sales and trading, asset management, private wealth management, and investment research). By continuously nurturing existing client relationships, growing new partnerships, and exploiting opportunities across the financial markets universe, the front-office divisions are able to continue to generate revenue for the investment bank each year. When one division performs poorly, there's usually another division that outperforms. As such, having a diverse range of divisions in the front office can offer the unique benefit of hedging (minimising risk) as a result of diversification.

Compensation

In general, compensation (i.e. base salaries and annual bonuses) tends to be higher in the front office compared to the middle office and the back office. This is due to the simple fact that front-office employees and divisions contribute directly to the revenue and profits of the investment bank. A few other factors that contribute to the demand for higher pay in front-office roles include the culture of working long hours, the intense working environments, the client-facing nature of the work, and the fierce competition for these roles.

Keep in mind that bonuses are performance based and can vary significantly from individual to individual, and from year to year. Performance-based bonuses depend on many factors, including individual performance, team performance, division-specific performance, overall firm performance, and, last but not least, the current financial market environment (you can generally expect better bonuses in a booming economy versus an economy in recession).

Work–Life Balance

Work–life balance in the front office can be challenging, especially during the first two to four years of your career. The culture of finance and banking careers expects junior professionals with front-office roles to work long hours. For example, the most gruelling of these is the investment banking division, where analysts can expect to work 80–100-hour weeks (that's five to six days of 15–18-hour shifts) for their first two years. The analysts on the trading floor, on the other hand, can expect to get into the office around 6 am and expect to leave anywhere between 6 pm and 9 pm. The front-office divisions that tend to provide the 'best' working hours are the asset management, investment research, and private wealth management businesses. Here you can expect 11–14-hour work days on average, as an entry-level analyst.

Working in these divisions can be particularly busy during certain times of the year, however. These include earnings seasons, deal closings, quarterly reporting, and periods of heightened market volatility.

As such, it's worth noting that careers which are less technical, such as sales and client relationship management, typically offer better work–life balance than more technical roles such as trading and portfolio management.

This is something worth thinking about when applying to roles and firms as it'll heavily dictate the extent to which you have a manageable work–life balance in your career. And while some roles offer more flexibility, the general expectation in the front office is a strong commitment to the role, often at the expense of tons of personal time.

Breaking In

Generally speaking, breaking into an investment bank is tough, but breaking into a front-office role is even tougher. This is due to the extremely high competition for a handful of open positions. In any given year, Goldman Sachs will typically receive more than 200,000 applications for its 3,500 summer internship positions. That's less than a 2% acceptance rate. The acceptance rate for graduate positions is even lower. On top of the high level of competition for these roles, the demand for specific skills, as well as the prestige associated with some of the investment banks, make these positions highly coveted.

The candidates who often secure offers for front-office roles tend to have a strong academic record, attend a prestigious university, have a handful of relevant internships, and have a number of impressive extracurricular activities, voluntary experiences, and hobbies/interests. Last but not least, the selection process for identifying the ideal and best candidates is rigorous, with multiple rounds of interviews and assessments (these can range from firm to firm, but you should expect a battery of online tests, an online interview, an in-person assessment centre, and at least one in-person interview).

As daunting as this may all seem, it isn't uncommon for firms to hire candidates who don't display any or all of the above. So, rest assured, you don't necessarily need to go to an elite university to break in. A lot of candidates from non-traditional backgrounds are securing offers for front-office roles, now more than ever.

Breaking In from the Middle Office or Back Office

It's possible to move from the middle or the back office into the front office; however, it's easier said than done. There are two main factors that determine one's likelihood of moving into the front office from a middle or back-office division.

The first is whether you're working in a division that's closely tied to the front-office division of interest. For example, if you work in human resources or audit, the chances of moving into the front office are unlikely because the work you currently do isn't related to the work you would be doing in the front office. To add to that, your current role doesn't facilitate any interaction with the desired division you might want to move into within the front office. Two divisions where this wouldn't be the case include risk management and operations. These two divisions work directly with the front office and need to have a strong understanding of their work. As such, a natural connection exists which can be leveraged to explore potential opportunities for a move to the front office.

The second factor is all about consistently outperforming and impressing the people whom you interact and work with from the front office. You simply want to build a strong reputation and gain the recognition you deserve as a reliable and capable pair of hands. Furthermore, top-quartile performers are more likely to impress and be accepted for interviews in the front office as opposed to middle or bottom-quartile employees. Therefore, if you're considering making a move, be sure to have strong performance for a year or two first.

Other ways of increasing the odds of a move into the front office include building and leveraging a strong internal network, and gaining the relevant skills and knowledge to succeed in the role via courses and qualifications such as a relevant Master's degree, MBA, or certifications like the CFA (Chartered Financial Analyst) or FRM (Financial Risk Manager).

Education and Qualifications

Although it's true that you can break into the front office having studied a non-finance-related degree, or without doing a Master's degree, it most definitely strengthens your application if you've done a finance-related degree or have a finance-related Master's. This is particularly true for the more finance-focused and technical career paths. For example, STEM (Science, Technology, Engineering, and Mathematics) degrees are generally preferred for technical roles such as trading, quantitative trading or research, structuring, and so on. Furthermore, the undergraduate studying an accounting degree will be better suited for an investment banking internship where they'll be expected to analyse and research the financial statements of companies as opposed to the undergraduate studying a social sciences degree, for example. Having said this, some teams prefer non-finance graduates in order to welcome the potential benefits of diversity of thought and thinking. As such, we have to take the previous examples with a little caution as they'll always have their own nuances and should be considered on a case-by-case basis. Notwithstanding, your educational background and degree discipline can play an important role in getting through the application process.

Should you wish to stand out further, you can (and should most definitely) consider doing an industry or role-specific qualification. A classic example in the world of finance, particularly in asset management, would be spending time doing a qualification such as the CFA or the IMC (Investment Management Certificate). In the world of asset management, most professionals on the technical side (portfolio managers and product specialists) as well as salespeople (client relationship managers) will be expected to dedicate the required time (typically three years for the three levels of the CFA) to attain the highly recognised and established qualification. Essentially, anyone with the CFA is recognised as an individual with a strong knowledge of financial concepts used across the investing landscape, particularly in fund management (asset management). Having this qualification, or even preparing for level 1 as an undergraduate, shows a great deal of initiative and can easily make you stand out in applications and interviews.

Advanced degrees such as an MBA from a top-tier business school can also open many doors to front-office positions, especially in investment banking. The downside of MBAs, however, is that they're often very expensive.

Career Opportunities and Networking

In the front office, networking and building strong professional relationships can have a significant impact on your career trajectory. These connections can be developed through attending industry events, building strong relationships with clients, or seeking out mentors and sponsors within your company. Think about it, it's much easier to be accepted for an interview if a mutual connection has recommended and vouched for you, as opposed to applying cold (without a warm introduction).

Having a strong reputation will serve you well in the world of finance. After all, it's a small world out there and across the industry you're only a few connections away from everyone. Most people will know someone that knows you, and vice versa. As such, it's important to keep this in mind when pursuing new opportunities and it's also important to keep this in mind when seeking to connect with specific industry professionals.

ASSET MANAGEMENT

All over the world, corporations, governments, sovereign wealth funds, charities, pension funds, insurance companies, and other large organisations have money that needs to be managed and invested. This money needs to be managed or invested by experts in order to either retain or grow its value. This is where the world of asset management (also referred to as fund management and investment management) comes in.

Asset management is the business of managing and investing capital on behalf of clients (institutions, corporations, etc.) in order to achieve a desired outcome set out by the client. This outcome is typically determined by the circumstances, risk appetite, goals, and objectives of the client in question. For example, the time frame for investing the money, as well as the risk appetite of the client, will heavily influence the way the money is invested into the financial markets.

Clients of Asset Managers

When we think about the clients of asset managers, they tend to fall into the following categories:

- pension funds
- insurance companies
- governments
- sovereign wealth funds
- local authorities
- endowments and foundations
- charities
- third-party distribution

You might be familiar with some of these terms, and not so familiar with others. In any case, let's break them down and why they'd need the services of an investment manager (asset management firm).

Pension funds are large pools of money put aside by companies or governments in order to provide retirement income to their employees. They need asset managers in order to invest this pool of money as efficiently and appropriately as possible, so as to meet future pension obligations. Asset managers are able to help pension funds manage their risk and return by investing across a diversified range of asset classes and building a diversified portfolio for the pension fund over time.

Insurance companies manage large sums of money that people and companies pay them in order to cover any future claims. Once again, they need asset managers to invest these reserves in case their customers (policyholders) make any insurance claims. Asset managers help insurance companies balance their need for liquidity, income generation, and capital preservation. Asset managers tend to invest a large portion of insurance client capital into the fixed-income markets to align with the predictable payout structures of insurance products.

Governments might use asset managers to invest excess funds or manage sovereign wealth. For example, asset managers help governments achieve objectives such as funding public services, infrastructure projects like building roads and bridges, and stabilising the economy during a recession or economic downturn.

Sovereign wealth funds are state-owned investment funds that are used to manage a country's reserves. They need asset managers to invest in a diversified portfolio that ensures long-term capital preservation and growth.

Local authorities, or local councils, manage public funds for services like community projects, education, and infrastructure. Asset managers help local authorities invest their capital in order to ensure they meet their financial obligations whilst also preserving capital.

Endowments (investment funds) and foundations (non-profit organisations) need management of their funds in order to support their operations and charitable missions. They hire asset managers to ensure the long-term growth and sustainability of their funds. Once again, asset managers help these organisations by investing in diversified portfolios that generate income whilst preserving capital and minimising risk.

Charities tend to manage funds to support their philanthropic goals and missions. They need asset managers to help maximise the impact of donations and grants by investing in prudent investment strategies. Charities will typically have ethical requirements to ensure their investments are aligned with their charity values. For example, medical/health charities may say they don't want to invest in tobacco or alcohol companies, or environmental charities may not invest in oil and gas companies. As such, asset managers are able to create custom portfolios that cater to these specific needs.

Third parties, or third-party distribution, refers to financial intermediaries, such as financial advisors and wealth managers. These individuals and firms often distribute asset management products that meet the diverse needs of their clients (usually individual and institutional investors). They rely on asset managers to create and build expertly managed investment portfolios and products so that they can promote and sell them on to their own list of clients.

Roles in Asset Management

There are broadly three main categories of roles or careers you can pursue in asset management:

- sales (salespeople, client relationship managers, consultant relations professionals)
- investment (traders, portfolio managers, product specialists, etc.)
- support (operations team, marketing team, human resources professionals)

Let's dig a little deeper into the specific responsibilities and expectations that come with each of these roles.

Portfolio managers lead the investment side of asset management. They're responsible for making important investment decisions and managing the risk within portfolios in order to achieve a specific financial goal for the firms' clients. Portfolio managers are expected to constantly monitor the financial markets and analyse market trends, economic data, and individual securities in order to construct and maintain a diversified portfolio. They're constantly rebalancing portfolios and making adjustments based on what's going on across the financial markets in order to better cater to their clients' needs. They focus on a specific asset class. For example, there are portfolio managers who only manage equity portfolios, and there are portfolio managers who only manage fixed-income portfolios. This is the norm across the industry.

Salespeople and *client relationship managers* focus on bringing in new business for the firm whilst also nurturing existing relationships with the firm's current clients. Client relationship managers in particular are responsible for ensuring all client needs, requests, and demands are met, whilst salespeople spend most of their time prospecting (building new relationships) and pitching (selling, presenting, and promoting the firm's products to potential clients). These roles are crucial for client retention and business development, as strong client relationships often lead to increased client satisfaction and growth of assets invested with the asset manager. Salespeople and client relationship managers work closely with portfolio managers and product specialists in order to develop their understanding of complex products, work together on client pitches, and ensure the best products are put forward to meet any given client's investment needs.

Consultant relations professionals manage relationships with investment consultants. Who are investment consultants? Well, firms like Aon Hewitt, Willis Towers Watson, KPMG, and Hymans Robertson, for example, all have consultants who specialise in investments. The clients of asset managers such as pension schemes are encouraged (sometimes required) to have an investment consultant working with them. The investment consultant will usually carry out an extensive review and research (due diligence) into the various products that the asset manager has on offer and share a rating for each. They'll then advise the client (pension fund, insurance company, etc.) on these product reviews and whether they would or wouldn't advise investing in them. As such, there needs to be a dedicated team in asset management firms that's responsible for building and managing relationships with these technical investment consultants. That's where the consultant relations team comes in.

As the name suggests, *product specialists* are experts in a particular investment product or asset class. They're responsible for creating products and educating clients and colleagues on the details of such products. Product specialists tend to specialise in specific niches. For example, within equities there are subsectors such as technology stocks, healthcare stocks, large-cap stocks, and small-cap stocks. As such, most large asset managers will have product specialists who cover multiple companies within each of these subsectors.

Let's use the fixed-income asset class as another example. Within fixed income there are subsectors such as high-yield, emerging markets, municipalities, government debt, and more. These will all have product specialists focusing only on each subsector or category. This structure is pretty consistent across all of the asset classes. Firms have product specialists working on different subsectors within each asset class. As well as becoming experts on a particular niche, product specialists work closely with portfolio managers and sales teams to develop, manage, and promote specific investment products. The product specialists' nature of work can range from working on product presentations to preparing Excel spreadsheets with detailed interpreted data, graphs, and charts.

Traders in asset management are execution traders only. They're different from traders in sales and trading since they don't make markets (i.e. connect buyers and sellers in order to take a transaction fee or commission). They buy and sell orders for financial securities on behalf of the firm or its clients, based on the strategies that suit and meet the needs of the given fund or portfolio in question. Traders are expected to monitor the financial markets, especially the parts of the markets that most impact the asset class they're covering, manage trade execution, and ensure compliance with all relevant regulatory requirements. If you want to be a trader, you'll need to be comfortable working under pressure, be a great decision-maker, and have a strong desire for learning about the financial markets and how they're impacted. One of the key skills of a good trader is being able to execute trades at the best possible price as this directly impacts the potential returns and performance of investment portfolios.

The *operations team* in asset management is responsible for the essential administrative and logistical tasks that ensure the firm's sales and investing personnel are able to operate as efficiently as possible. They handle everything from trade settlements and back-end client account management to ensuring compliance with both regulatory standards and internal policies. Working in operations is kind of like working in the engine room of the business. You'll be constantly improving systems and working on projects to ensure salespeople, portfolio managers, and traders are able to focus on serving clients and making the right investment decisions. Without operations employees, trades could go wrong, client funds could easily be misused or lost, and the business would simply fall apart.

The *marketing team* plays a key role in promoting the firm's brand, products, and services, all with the goal of attracting and retaining clients. They're responsible for designing marketing materials, strategies, and managing the firm's online presence (website, social media, etc.). A big part of the role in marketing is understanding client needs and staying on top of industry trends through thorough market research. As such, marketing teams work closely with salespeople and client relationship managers as they can often be heavily involved in client-specific projects, events, and roadshows.

Human resource professionals in asset management are responsible for all things relating to the most important asset within any organisation: the employees. From campus recruitment efforts to developing and retaining top talent within the organisation, they ensure that the firm complies with labour laws and maintains a positive work environment. Human resources is crucial in shaping the company's culture and making sure the firm attracts and keeps the top talent required for each of the sales, investment, and support areas within the firm.

INVESTMENT BANKING

The investment banking division is often seen as the pinnacle of careers at investment banks. It's the division of the investment bank that requires the longest working hours (expect 14–18-hour days, five or six days a week for your first two years as an analyst) and often pays the highest total compensation (base salary and bonus). From a commercial perspective, the investment banking division plays a crucial role in the world of finance and provides a range of services to clients across industries, of different sizes, and located all over the world.

Investment banking is all about helping clients (corporations, governments, large institutions, etc.) raise capital, manage risks, and execute complex transactions such as mergers (where two companies merge and join forces) and acquisitions (where one company acquires or takes over another). You can split the nature of investment banking into two main categories: financial advisory and capital markets.

Financial advisory focuses on advising companies on the most suitable ways in which to manage risk, restructure a business or organisation, and other corporate strategy advice. In contrast, capital markets, or capital raising, focuses on identifying the best options for raising capital for a company through the debt and equity markets. When we talk about raising money through the debt or equity markets, all we mean is raising money by borrowing money or taking out loans on a large scale (debt), or raising money by selling shares of a company (equity).

Industry Groups and Product Groups

It's worth knowing that investment banking divisions are, for the most part, organised into industry groups and product groups, each with a unique focus. These groups work together in order to service the firm's clients and execute financial transactions successfully. Understanding the differences between the industry and product groups is imperative if you're interested in breaking into investment banking specifically. Having a solid understanding of the similarities and differences between the two groups will enable you to make an informed decision when it comes to deciding which area is more suitable for you and your career goals.

Industry Groups

Industry groups, also known as sector groups, focus on specific industries or sectors of the economy. If you're working in an industry group at an investment bank, your primary aim is to develop a deep knowledge of a particular industry, say technology, for example. This deep expertise will then allow you to add value to clients with industry-specific insights. Working in the industry group is all about building long-term relationships with clients across the sector you're specialising in, so that you can be the first point of contact should they ever seek any financial advisory services.

Investment bankers working in industry groups typically have three main responsibilities:

- developing their industry expertise
- building and nurturing client relationships
- deal sourcing

Let's go through these individually.

Developing industry expertise is all about staying up-to-date on industry trends, understanding the inner workings and value drivers within the industry, and providing tailored advice based on one's existing and extensive knowledge of the sector.

Building and nurturing client relationships is the exercise of continuously prospecting (exploring and searching for new clients) whilst keeping existing client relationships warm and progressive. Many companies that work with investment banks once tend to use the same investment bank in the future as and when the need arises. As such, it makes sense to keep a continuous dialogue and maintain regular interaction with these companies/clients.

Last but not least, *deal sourcing* requires investment bankers to regularly keep an eye out for potential deals that the firm can work on, or at least put their name in the hat for. Deal sourcing is all about identifying new opportunities and is often made easier by building an extensive network of industry contacts (something that grows with time and experience).

A few of the most common industry groups include Technology, Media, and Telecom (TMT), Healthcare, Financial Institutions Group (FIG), Energy & Natural Resources, Consumer & Retail, and Industrials. If you're keen on breaking into an industry group, it's always a good idea to identify which industry fascinates you the most and then build your knowledge around trends, deals, and so on that are happening within that industry. This is an extremely simple way to stand out in interviews and applications.

Product Groups

Product groups, on the other hand, focus on the different types of products or transactions that the firm offers. Individuals in product groups are responsible for executing deals and providing technical expertise across a wide range of industries (unlike the industry group bankers who only focus on one industry). Bankers in product groups tend to be more technical as they focus a lot more on the structuring and executing of complex financial products and transactions.

Investment bankers working in product groups typically have three main responsibilities:

- transaction execution
- technical expertise
- cross-industry collaboration

Let's go through these individually.

Transaction execution is all about successfully executing on deals such as M&A transactions, debt issuances, equity issuances, and restructuring. As such, transaction execution requires closely working with industry group colleagues to ensure deals are structured in the best possible way.

Technical expertise requirements for investment banking include being an expert in financial modelling (using Microsoft Excel to develop models with the aim of predicting the value of companies for various purposes), deal structuring (identifying the optimal mix of debt and equity when raising capital for a client), and navigating regulatory requirements (keeping up-to-date on new regulations is vital to avoid breaking any laws).

Lastly, *cross-industry collaboration* means that product group bankers work with, and therefore are exposed to, clients from all industries. While industry group bankers bring in deals and manage client relationships (you can think of this part of their role as salespeople), product group bankers mostly step in to take care of the technical execution of the transactions.

The most common product groups include:

- M&A, which is responsible for advising companies on buying, selling, or merging with other companies for a strategic benefit.
- ECM (Equity Capital Markets), which is responsible for raising money for clients through the equity markets, such as through an initial public offering (IPO, i.e. offering shares of the company to

institutional investors or the general public), secondaries (selling shares in a secondary market such as from one investor to another), or private placements (selling shares to a pre-selected and pre-vetted list of buyers).

- DCM (Debt Capital Markets), which is responsible for helping clients raise money through the debt markets, such as through loans and other debt instruments.
- Leveraged Finance, which specialises in highly risky transactions that use a lot of debt in order to lever up (maximise the earning potential) of a potential investment.
- Restructuring, which is responsible for advising companies that are facing financial hardship or challenges on the best way to tackle the given situation by helping them restructure their debt, negotiate with creditors, or avoid bankruptcy.

SALES AND TRADING

The trading floor, otherwise known as the sales and trading division or global markets, is the part of an investment bank that you've probably seen or heard about the most. It's the part of the business that tends to be the focal point of most finance movies, think *The Wolf of Wall Street* and *The Big Short*, given the intense nature and high pressure of the trading floor, and the all-too-common grandiose and direct personalities that one can expect to find there.

From a commercial point of view, the sales and trading division plays a core function within investment banks and is typically a large contributor to the revenue generated by the firm each year. You can think of the big three divisions being investment banking, sales and trading, and investment management (asset management and private wealth management). These divisions tend to bring in the bulk of the firm's revenue each year, however, in tough markets it's common that revenue generation for the year will fluctuate for each of these businesses.

In terms of what the sales and trading business actually does, it essentially facilitates the buying and selling of financial instruments (stocks, bonds, currencies, commodities, derivatives, etc.) on behalf of the firm's clients, and in some cases for the firm's own account. This is otherwise known as market-making. The traders are making a market by connecting both buyers and sellers of financial assets to come together and trade. Without this market it would have been fairly impossible for the buyer to have come across the seller, and, as such, the trader takes a fee or a commission for making the transaction happen. A common misconception is that the sales and trading division is buying and selling financial securities for its own account and in order to make a profit from successfully trading the securities across the financial markets. This is called proprietary trading and is more common at hedge funds as opposed to the trading floors of investment banks. As such, the primary form of revenue generation for the sales and trading division of an investment bank is through commissions or fees for market-making.

To put it into perspective, taking a small percentage from thousands of multi-million-dollar transactions can quickly add up, and this is why the sales and trading division contributes billions in annual revenue to most bulge bracket investment banks.

From a cultural perspective, the trading floor isn't for the faint of heart. It's an extremely high-pressure, fast paced, and intense working environment that requires quick thinking, deep market knowledge, and extremely strong analytical skills. It's also one of the most dynamic areas of the investment bank, with market conditions constantly changing and, as such, requiring individuals within the business to quickly adapt to new information. You'll come across big personalities on the trading floor, and the culture tends to be direct and no-nonsense as opposed to patient and forgiving. This all makes sense given the nature of the business.

Clients of the Trading Floor

The sales and trading division's clients tend to be quite similar to those of the asset management business, and so it isn't uncommon for these two divisions of an investment bank to cover the same clients but offer a different service to them. For example, the asset management division will most likely be managing a client's long-term investment portfolio, whilst the sales and trading division would be taking care of its more immediate and short-term trading needs.

More specifically, these clients can include sovereign wealth funds, endowments and foundations, insurance companies, pension funds, high-net-worth individuals, corporations, hedge funds, investment banks, and other large institutional investors.

Each client will have a different set of needs and objectives, and it's up to the sales and trading division to tailor their services to meet these specific requirements. For example, a large airline company might use the sales and trading division to hedge (protect) its exposure to fluctuating oil prices by entering into a long-term contract for fuel at a fixed price. In contrast, a family office or high-net-worth individual might invest with a greater focus on wealth preservation, generating a steady stream of income, and minimising potential tax liabilities.

Roles on the Trading Floor

Although the division itself is called the sales and trading division, there are a number of career paths within the division that all play a key role in the division's success. These roles include:

- salespeople
- traders
- sales-traders
- research analysts and economists

- quantitative analysts (more commonly known as quants)
- structurers

Let's briefly run through what each of these roles entails.

Salespeople are the face of the business. They're responsible for developing, maintaining, and managing relationships with clients of the division. They act as the primary point of contact for clients, and are expected to tend to any inbound requests, proposals, or client-specific needs as and when they arise. As a salesperson on the trading floor, you'll be expected to provide your clients with market updates, offer investment ideas, and often facilitate trades for them. At its core, the salesperson's role is all about understanding what any given client wants or needs and catering to it with the most suitable and appropriate financial products or trading strategies. If you like the idea of being on the phone with clients for most of your day, pitching ideas, analysing and discussing what's going on in the markets, and working closely with traders, then this might be a suitable role for you.

Traders are responsible for generating trade ideas and executing buy-and-sell orders on behalf of the firm and its clients. Given that financial markets are extremely dynamic and constantly changing, the frequent movement in prices of financial instruments can have significant implications on the outcomes of trades that traders execute. As such, a large part of a trader's role is focused on risk management and ensuring that trades are completed at the best possible price. For those of you interested in this line of work, you'll need to have a passion for the markets, strong analytical skills and attention to detail, the ability to think fast on your feet, and most importantly, the ability to not just work well, but thrive under intense pressure.

Sales-traders, as the name suggests, are a kind of hybrid between a salesperson and a trader. They act as a kind of bridge between the salespeople and traders, whilst ensuring that client orders are executed efficiently and at the best possible price. The difference between sales-traders and salespeople is that the sales-trader has the ability to execute trades whereas the salesperson is purely acting in a relationship management or pitching capacity.

And the difference between the sales-trader and traders is that traders usually have no client interaction responsibilities, but sales-traders do.

Research analysts and economists support the sales and trading division by carrying out in-depth research on a specific market, asset, or financial security and sharing their findings with the broader trading floor (most importantly with the salespeople and the traders). In these roles you can expect to produce research reports, market updates, and investment recommendations for the salespeople, traders, and even clients to use. If you like the idea of spending most of your days analysing financial data, writing research reports, and presenting your findings as investment recommendations, then this might be a suitable role for you.

Quantitative analysts, otherwise known as quants, are specialists in leveraging the use of data, mathematical models, and algorithms to develop unique trading strategies. On the trading floor, quants work closely with traders to try to create and refine algorithms that can allow traders to execute trades more effectively and efficiently, and sometimes even automatically. In the world of trading, speed is everything. As such, having an edge when it comes to the speed with which you can trade or capture trades at specific prices can be hugely beneficial and profitable for the firm. Being a quant is a highly technical and detail-oriented profession. This career requires you to be comfortable with risk management, statistical analysis, and other complex and technical responsibilities. If you're interested in this type of role, it's worth knowing that most quants typically have a background in a highly technical degree such as physics, mathematics, engineering, or statistics.

PRIVATE WEALTH MANAGEMENT

Private wealth management is similar to asset management in that it focuses on managing and investing money for its clients. The key differentiator between the two divisions is the clientele. In asset management, clients are large institutional investors, corporates, and governmental organisations. In contrast, the clients of private wealth management divisions are typically high-net-worth individuals and families.

If you haven't already, you'll likely come across the term 'private banking'. Whenever you hear this term, it's safe to assume that the context and usage is also referring to private wealth management. However, it's worth noting that although the terms are often used interchangeably, they aren't the exact same in terms of what they offer. A simple way to think about the two is to see private banking as a subset of private wealth management. For example, private banking doesn't always include investing, whereas private wealth management does. To add to that, private wealth management takes a more holistic approach and offers clients a broader range of financial and wealth management services, including tax planning, investing, insurance, estate planning, inheritance planning, and more.

Private wealth management is a highly personal business where professionals are responsible for managing and growing their clients' wealth through a combination of investment strategies, estate planning, risk management, and tax optimisation. If you're interested in working in the world of private wealth management, a primarily relationship-driven business, it's important to have strong interpersonal skills whilst also being comfortable with meeting new people and building long-term relationships. After all, you'll be responsible for managing the financial lives of your clients, which goes beyond simply managing investments.

Clients of Private Wealth Managers

It's safe to assume that the clients of private banks and private wealth management divisions of investment banks have wealth. However, there are different levels of wealth and this is what separates the clients in this business. Essentially, there are three main types of clients:

- high-net-worth individuals (HNWIs)
- ultra-high-net-worth individuals (UHNWIs)
- family offices

HNWIs are individuals with investable assets typically in the region of $1 million to $30 million. These clients often include successful entrepreneurs, corporate executives, sports professionals, athletes, and inheritors of family wealth.

UHNWIs, on the other hand, are individuals with investable assets exceeding $30 million. This group often includes billionaires, celebrities, large business owners, royals, and members of extremely wealthy families.

Family offices are private companies that manage the wealth of a single wealthy family with the aim of preserving the family's wealth for future generations.

Roles in Private Wealth Management

Private wealth management offers a range of roles for graduates and professionals to look into and consider ahead of working in the industry. These include:

- wealth managers or private bankers
- investment advisors
- financial planners
- client service associates

Let's go through these one by one.

A *wealth manager* or *private banker* is the primary point of contact for clients. They usually have at least a decade's worth of experience under their belt and are responsible for managing the firm's most important client relationships, understanding these clients' financial goals, and developing comprehensive financial plans for them.

Next, you have the *investment advisor*, who focuses on the more technical aspects of private wealth management. Investment advisors are responsible for managing the investment portfolios of clients. If you enjoy the idea of conducting research, analysing markets and trends, and making recommendations on how best to allocate assets, then this is the role for you.

A *financial planner* is responsible for developing a long-term strategy focusing on the financial plans of clients, with a particular focus on areas such as retirement planning, estate planning, and tax optimisation.

Client service associates are junior professionals whose primary role is to support wealth managers and investment advisors by taking care of administrative tasks, client communications, and account management. The typical progression route for client service associates after a few years is to progress up the hierarchy of either the wealth management career path (more client-focused and less technical) or the investment advisory path (more technical and less client-focused).

If you're interested in breaking into the world of private wealth management, I encourage you to start thinking of ways that you can build up your experience around customer service, interpersonal skills, and investment and financial markets knowledge.

INVESTMENT RESEARCH

The investment research division is the division within an investment bank that's most suitable for you if you enjoy writing essays and carrying out research on a particular topic. This division is responsible for delivering in-depth analysis and insights that contribute to investment decisions for institutional and retail investors. Investment research is broad and has roles across all of the different asset classes and sectors. This includes having research analysts covering equities, bonds, commodities, alternative investments, and beyond. Essentially, the end goal or purpose of investment research is to equip the firm itself as well as its clients with detailed, actionable recommendations so they can make well-informed investment decisions.

Investment research analysts spend most of their time examining financial data, market trends, and economic indicators in order to identify potential opportunities or issues. Most tend to specialise in a specific sector, such as technology, healthcare, and so on, or on asset classes like fixed income or equities. Once they've carried out their research, they produce highly detailed in-depth research reports that often include 'buy', 'sell', or 'hold' recommendations. These reports are extremely important to asset managers and investors who rely on up-to-date insights to help them drive profitable investment decisions.

If you're a junior professional in this division, you can expect to take care of all the data gathering and basic analysis. The more senior you become, the more exposure you'll have to forecasting, modelling, and client presentations. You'll also really get to know the companies you cover by meeting with their C-suite executives, going to their production facilities, testing their products, and really getting an under-the-hood view of how they operate. Useful skills to break into the world of research include financial modelling, valuation techniques, and quantitative analysis.

One key distinction is that the world of research is often split into sell-side and buy-side research teams, each with its own focus. Sell-side analysts (usually at investment banks) produce research for external clients like hedge funds, mutual funds, and retail investors. Buy-side analysts work within asset management firms, using their research to improve and benefit the firm's internal investment portfolios. Unlike sell-side research, buy-side research is usually kept for internal use only.

If you have a genuine interest in a particular sector or segment of the financial markets, enjoy carrying out in-depth research and report writing, understanding how the world around you impacts particular industries, and can see yourself doing this type of work for 10–12 hours a day, then investment research is a career worth considering.

MIDDLE OFFICE

The middle-office divisions are the backbone of any financial institution, working closely with the front office and the back office to ensure smooth and efficient operations throughout the firm. While the middle office doesn't directly contribute to revenue generation like the front office does, the middle office plays a critical role in risk management, treasury services, and operations. Each of these divisions have both middle-office and back-office functionalities and teams. However, for this section of this chapter let's focus on their roles within the middle office.

Risk Management

Middle-office risk management is the part of the bank that deals with monitoring, assessing, and controlling risks that relate directly to the front-office divisions. As such, middle-office risk teams will most often focus on market risk, credit risk, and operational risk, and manage these risks proactively in order to ensure as close to real-time risk management as possible.

Examples of the work and tasks that you might do in these roles include setting risk limits so that portfolios or trades don't accidentally exceed the level of risk the firm or clients are willing to take on, conducting scenario analysis (i.e. using technology and programmes to create 'what if' situations and seeing how investment portfolios might react in such situations), and then using this information to make investment decisions, stress testing (i.e. testing the limits of firms and portfolios), and generating reports that help the front office make informed, risk-adjusted decisions.

For example, market risk analysts might track the firm's exposures in trading activities in order to ensure that the trading activities are aligned with the firm's risk appetite and regulatory requirements, while credit risk analysts will be responsible for assessing counterparty risks (the risks associated with working with particular firms or clients) in order to prevent potential defaults such as failure to pay or keeping up their side of the deal.

Treasury Services

Treasury services are all about monitoring and managing the firm's own financial risks, which include interest-rate risk and currency risk. The purpose of managing these risks is to ensure that the firm has sufficient liquidity and funding to run its day-to-day operations. Imagine for a moment that an investment bank didn't have the cash flow to run its operations and divisions. The whole firm would come to a standstill as the divisions would fail to operate. The disruption in cash-flow management would impact employees and salaries, payments, and invoices that need to be sent to clients, borrowing and lending costs due to insufficient funds which impact the interest rates and currency conversion rates the firm will and will not be able to take advantage of, and so much more.

And so, the treasury services division exists in order to ensure this never happens. If you work in a middle-office treasury services role you can expect to work on any of the following: risk management, cash-flow forecasting, or strategic financial planning.

Essentially, the crux of your role will be to ensure an optimum capital allocation, manage the cost of funding, and advise on investment strategies for any surplus cash that exists in the business. By having this type of strategic oversight, you're playing an active role in ensuring that the firm's liquidity and financial risks are managed in alignment with its needs and broader financial strategy.

Operations

Oftentimes, you might hear about the operations division and immediately assume 'back office'. However, similar to the risk management and treasury functions within investment banks, the operations division has roles that are more middle-office focused, such as being in close proximity to the front-office daily work, and some that are more back-office focused, with less interaction with the front-office divisions.

Middle-office operations roles predominantly focus on roles such as trade support, risk management, and any other activities that ensure the smooth processes for front-office divisions. Such tasks often involve verifying and confirming the details of trades, trade reconciliation (when trade transaction sizes are in the hundreds of thousands to millions of dollars, it's worth having a separate team double-checking that everything adds up and is correct), monitoring risk exposure, and managing operational risks associated with transactions such as insufficient client funds, external fraud risk, cybersecurity risk, and so on.

To summarise, middle-office operations acts as an important layer of support and defence between the front office and the back office by ensuring that trades and investments are accurately processed, recorded, and aligned with the regulatory requirements the firm is expected to abide by.

BACK OFFICE

The back office is like the engine room of the investment bank. It has all the divisions that keep the business up and running behind the scenes. Whilst back-office functions aren't responsible for revenue generation, and aren't interacting with front-office divisions like the middle-office divisions do, they're still extremely important. The front and middle offices focus on client-facing roles and risk management, for the most part, while the back office takes care of the day-to-day processing, record-keeping, legal, accounting, technological, and administrative functions that support everything happening across all levels of the firm. In addition, since the work isn't as demanding or revenue-focused, they have shorter working hours and offer a better work–life balance compared to the front office. However, back-office roles tend to offer lower base salaries and lower compensation packages. With all this in mind, let's go through each of the back-office functions. Keep in mind that some of these (risk management, treasury services, operations, and compliance) were also covered in the Middle Office section, given that they have roles spanning both the middle and back office.

Risk Management

Whilst the middle-office risk management teams are focused on monitoring, controlling, and assessing risks related to front-office divisions, back-office risk management is typically more supportive and administrative in nature. It involves activities like data gathering, record-keeping, regulatory reporting, and audit preparation to document the firm's compliance with risk-management policies.

Essentially, back-office risk management teams are tasked with ensuring that the firm's risk-management processes meet regulatory standards, and they might also help with risk-mitigation efforts through internal audits, compliance checks, and process improvements.

Treasury Services

Whilst the middle-office treasury services roles are tasked with monitoring and managing the firm's own financial risks, back-office treasury services take care of all the transactional and administrative tasks, such as processing payments, managing daily cash positions, reconciling bank accounts, and executing any settlements. As such, back-office treasury roles focus on ensuring the smooth operation of daily cash flows, manage intercompany funding transfers, and support cash management by maintaining detailed records of transactions and performing regulatory reporting.

Operations

Unlike middle-office operations, where roles focus on trade support, risk management, and prioritising the smooth functioning of the front office, back-office operations, on the other hand, are generally more focused on post-trade processes and administrative tasks, such as settlement, clearing, record-keeping, and data management. These types of roles ensure that once a trade is executed, it's properly settled and logged within the firm's internal systems and records. Back-office operations teams keep everything running as smoothly as possible by making sure that financial reporting, compliance documentation, and database maintenance are all done to an extremely high standard.

Compliance

Compliance is effectively the firm's main line of defence. Within compliance there are many roles, from ensuring that trade desks comply with internal risk limits to verifying that client onboarding meets regulatory requirements like KYC (know your client) and AML (anti-money laundering) and preventing potential compliance breaches as transactions occur. A large part of these teams' responsibility is to ensure real-time monitoring and regulatory adherence by the firm. However, for the most part, compliance tends to focus on post-trade and administrative functions, such as regulatory reporting, audit preparation, and record-keeping from a compliance standpoint. This includes preparing reports for regulatory authorities, maintaining documentation to demonstrate compliance with laws and internal policies, and conducting routine audits to ensure ongoing compliance. By doing so, the compliance division is ensuring that the firm is in good standing with regulatory bodies and fulfils all of its necessary duties and documentation expectations.

Legal

The legal division within an investment bank is the firm's division that's responsible for all legal aspects of the firm's operations. Their main objective is to protect the bank from legal risks and disputes, whilst also helping to structure deals and manage transactions in a legally sound way.

One of the main roles of the legal division is contract review and negotiation. Let's take the investment banking division, for example. Every single merger or acquisition that the investment bank works on will have some form of paperwork or contract that ties more than one party into it. As such, it's the legal division's responsibility to make sure that every contract that's signed by the firm (or representatives of the firm) is sound, in the bank's best interests, and void of any potential risks. The legal team will draft, review, negotiate, and suggest amendments to contracts with clients, vendors, and counterparties. This is all extremely important, especially in high-stakes transactions such as M&As, financing agreements, and trading contracts, where precise and accurate legal language can prevent major issues down the line.

The legal division is also heavily involved in regulatory compliance. As such, it's not uncommon for legal teams to work closely with compliance teams and vice versa. The legal division is responsible for keeping the bank on the right side of the law, whilst the compliance division is responsible for keeping abreast of the most recent laws (i.e. regulatory requirements, changes, and initiatives that banks must adhere to).

Other functions and responsibilities of the legal division include litigation management (helping the bank handle legal disputes) and providing advisory support to different divisions (offering insights on issues such as intellectual property, employment law, AML regulations, etc.). They're the go-to resource for all divisions across the bank for guidance through complex legal questions and play an important role in ensuring the bank's operations are protected from a legal perspective.

Finance

Whilst the treasury services division of an investment bank is concerned with managing and monitoring the firm's own financial risks, the finance division is concerned with managing the investment bank's finances and ensuring that the firm is operating in a financially healthy and transparent way. The finance division fundamentally tracks everything from revenue and expenses to budgeting and financial planning, in order to create detailed reports and financial statements that give the leadership of the firm a clear picture and insight into how the firm is currently performing from a profitability and cost perspective. With access to such data and information, the leadership team of the firm are able to make better-informed decisions around budgeting, capital allocation, and strategic investments or initiatives. In short, if you join the finance division, you'll be tasked with constantly keeping a close tab on the firm's numbers, making sense of what they mean, and presenting them in an easy-to-understand format for key decision-makers across the firm.

Audit

The audit division acts as the bank's internal quality assurance team, reviewing its operations to ensure accuracy, efficiency, and compliance with internal and external standards. Their role is to examine financial records, systems, and controls across the bank to identify any discrepancies, inefficiencies, or potential risks. The audit division is regularly assessing whether the bank is following processes correctly and according to industry standards.

In audit, you can expect to conduct internal and/or external audits. Internal audits, as the name suggests, focus on identifying issues that could disrupt the daily operations of the firm itself. On the other hand, external audits are often performed in collaboration with external regulatory bodies or third parties.

The audit division plays a crucial role in the firm's risk management strategy as it has the ability to identify potential issues before they become a problem. By making sure the bank is operating in as efficient and effective a way as possible, the audit division helps maintain trust and accountability within the firm.

Human Resources

The most important asset of any investment bank is its people. This is where the human resources (HR) division comes into play. Human resources is responsible for overseeing the full employee lifecycle, from recruitment and onboarding to training, professional development, performance management, and retention. Human resource professionals and teams are also responsible for developing diversity, equity, and inclusion (DE&I) programmes, designing policies and programmes that support a positive working environment such as performance reviews, benefits, wellness programmes, and more. They are responsible for overseeing compliance with labour laws and ensuring that the bank's workplace practices meet industry and legal standards.

Technology

The technology division has, in recent times, become a division at the forefront of many conversations. This is largely due to the fact that the rise and evolution of technology and demand for technology talent across all industries, not just banking, has increased. Technologists are in demand, and given the growth and success of big tech companies, startups, and scale-ups reaching billion-dollar valuations, and the sheer prominence of artificial intelligence, pursuing a career in technology has grown heavily in popularity. As a result, investment banks are finding it harder to attract the tech talent they once found pretty straightforward to employ. After all, why would you want to work in a back-office technology role at an investment bank where you'll be expected to wear a suit, work long hours, and take home a lower pay package compared to joining a big tech company like Google, Apple, or Facebook, or an exciting startup or scale-up, where you can dress how you want, enjoy a better work–life balance, and potentially earn more. As a result of this shift in interests and demand for technology talent, investment banks have, over the years, allowed their employees within the technology division to come into work in less formal attire and enjoy better salary packages.

In terms of what the technology division does and the role it plays within the investment bank, it's straightforward. They are the backbone of an investment bank's digital infrastructure, enabling every division to operate efficiently. Technology teams are constantly designing, implementing, and maintaining the software and hardware systems that the investment bank needs in order to operate. Whether it be a unique software programme or system that the traders use to execute trades, a client management platform salespeople use for client relationship management, the operations division uses to monitor transactions, or employees across the firm and regions use to chat to one another, the technology division is at the heart of it all. Now more than ever, there's a major focus on innovation and digital transformation, such as how the technology division can leverage new technologies like artificial intelligence, machine learning, and data analytics in order to further optimise the firm's operations and processes. Another area of critical importance is cybersecurity, which is all about protecting the investment bank's systems and data from breaches and threats.

In short, the technology division of an investment bank collaborates closely with other divisions in order to customise tools and create platforms that meet their specific needs, provides cybersecurity, ensures the bank has the technological capabilities to remain competitive in a fast-paced digital landscape amongst many of its competitors, and provides the tools to serve clients securely and effectively.

CHAPTER 6

ROLES, RESPONSIBILITIES, AND CAREER PROGRESSION

I wanted to include a chapter that whittles down the typical career progression path that's most common within the world of finance and banking careers. Oftentimes, students and graduates are well aware of the intern and analyst roles but unaware of the expectations and how they evolve as you climb further up the corporate ladder. As such, in this chapter I'll touch on the most common titles and career progression routes in the industry, the typical length of time it takes to move from one position to the next, factors that influence career progression, expectations and responsibilities at each position, and more. We'll start with the executive assistant function, followed by analysts, associates, vice presidents/executive directors, directors, managing directors, and partners. Each firm and division across the industry is different and will likely have its own unique career progression path, titles, and timelines in order to reach each title or position. As such, use this chapter as a guide to get to know the positions a little better and understand how the expectations on each employee change as their tenure within the industry increases.

EXECUTIVE ASSISTANT

Most students and graduates are oblivious to the fact that this role even exists. Every team within each front-office division has an executive assistant who's keeping the team functioning and organised, from an operational standpoint. A highly efficient executive assistant will increase any team's productivity and efficiency, and bring immense value to the team such that they become indispensable. Teams simply can't function without executive assistants. Now, you're probably wondering what on earth does an executive assistant actually do? In essence, an executive assistant works closely with senior leaders and their teams to manage schedules, coordinate meetings, arrange travel, and handle and manage a wide range of administrative tasks. They typically work nine to five and it's not uncommon for two executive assistants to split the workload between them each week, essentially working part-time.

Think of it like this, irrespective of whether you're working on the trading floor, in asset management, private wealth management, research, or investment banking, there'll always be internal meetings, external meetings, conferences, events, coffees with prospects and clients, and so on. These meetings often require meeting rooms to be booked; teas, coffees, biscuits, and sandwiches to be ordered; external venues to be booked; travel to and from the meetings to be organised (taxis, trains, flights, etc.); adjustments to be made and reflected in participant calendars should anything change or someone be unable to attend; processing employee expenses for reimbursement; conference call details to be included in meetings and calendars; and so much more. With an endless amount of scheduling, optimising, and administrative tasks that require the attention of each team, it makes sense to have a full-time employee dedicated to taking care of it all. As such, this is where executive assistants are needed and provide a meaningful and substantial contribution to each team.

They're also the gatekeepers to the most senior executives within teams. If you ever try to cold email a managing director or partner, chances are their executive assistant will see your message first. And then they'll check with the managing director or partner on how best to respond.

If you're ever considering pursuing a career as an executive assistant, some of the key skills firms will be looking for include strong organisational skills, communication skills, time management, an eye for detail, and the ability to work to a high standard under pressure.

With regard to career progression and eventually being promoted, it's important to understand that the executive assistant role isn't part of the traditional progression route within the world of finance and banking. For example, it's not common for an executive assistant to leave their role and pursue a career as a full-time analyst. Having said this, it's not impossible either. When I was at Goldman Sachs one of the executive assistants decided she wanted to eventually be an analyst on the team and so she put her mind to it, passed the IMC (Investment Management Certificate), worked hard, and eventually left the executive assistant role to become a full-time analyst.

ANALYST

The analyst position is the most junior full-time, year-round role within the industry. It's the title you'll assume after joining a graduate programme or breaking into the industry after you graduate from an undergraduate degree or Master's programme. It's the entry point into the world of banking and finance and is often considered the toughest role, in its own way, on the ladder. At this stage of your career you'll be working on multiple projects simultaneously and pulled in lots of different directions throughout the week. As such, you'll often find yourself overwhelmed with the sheer amount of work that has to be done.

What's worse is that you'll find it hard to turn work away, or even feel guilty, because every other analyst around you will be willing to push themselves to the limit in order to impress, develop, grow, and earn as large a bonus as possible at the end of the year. You'll realise that you've entered into a culture where long hours have been normalised and working late, eating dinners that the firm covers the cost of, and ordering a cab to take you home, also at the expense of the firm, are now all just part of your job.

As an analyst you're at the bottom of the food chain. You're responsible for the grunt work that nobody else has the time or energy to do. To be fair, everyone more senior than you has already put in their grunt work hours. The grunt work will vary from division to division but it's often the most laborious, repetitive, manually intensive, and often mind-numbing work that can range from formatting PowerPoint presentations to creating financial models, or analysing tons of data to assisting associates and vice presidents on projects.

However, just because you'll be doing lots of grunt work doesn't mean the work isn't valuable to clients, or useful for your career growth and development. It's in the grunt work that you develop and build your foundation in finance, the ability to work long hours, multitask, manage your time effectively, get things done, and, for lack of a better phrase, push yourself to the limits. Working in such an intense manner for hours on end over an extended period of time allows you to hone your technical capabilities, attention to detail, and develop the stamina to work through complex tasks under tight deadlines and high pressure. It's intense to say the least, but if you can survive and progress past the analyst years, irrespective of how dull the work might be at times, and build a strong reputation for being a trusted pair of hands when something needs to get done, you'll be well prepared for a promotion to the next level up, associate.

The typical time frame to climb from analyst to associate ranges from firm to firm, but is often anywhere between two and four years. Some firms have a senior analyst position, whereas others move directly from analyst to associate. What matters when it comes to promotions is your ability to perform well throughout the years and rank in the top quartile in your end-of-year reviews. Doing so, as well as having strong reviews and feedback from your colleagues and manager, will enable you to climb the corporate ladder accordingly.

ASSOCIATE

Once you've mastered your role as an analyst and have built the confidence and proven your ability to take on more responsibility, you'll be promoted to the associate level. In all honesty, before you're promoted to any rank you'll likely have been operating at that level for at least six months already. Although it might feel like a big change given the new rank attached to your name, your new base salary, your higher status, and a new title added to your LinkedIn profile, you'll likely operate as you have been but with a few more expectations and goals agreed upon between both you and your manager.

As an associate you'll be taking on more responsibility compared to your time as an analyst. In this role, you're now going to be expected to start building your people skills further by managing and reviewing the work of those more junior to you (i.e. the analysts and possibly any interns on the team). You'll also be expected to handle and take care of more complex work-related matters, whether they be financial modelling, trading, client or business related. If you're in a sales role you'll start to explore building your own book of business, and you'll do so by taking the lead on your own meetings and hosting clients independently, whereas previously you might have been taken to meetings to take notes as an analyst.

In essence, as an associate you'll be expected to develop your technical skills and start taking on more leadership responsibilities within your team in order to ensure projects are completed to a high standard and any client's or prospect's expectations are met.

Moving from associate to vice president/executive director level is all about proving that you can not just handle the responsibilities that come with managing one analyst or improving your technical skills, but also have the ability to manage a whole team of analysts and associates as well as continually improving from a commercial and/or technical perspective. This usually takes anywhere from two to four years depending on ability, division, and firm.

VICE PRESIDENT/ EXECUTIVE DIRECTOR

Naturally, the higher you climb in the world of banking and finance, the less grunt work you'll be doing, but the more commercial and business or revenue-generating contributions will be expected of you (particularly in the front office). The higher you climb, the less hours you'll tend to work, but the decisions you make will have a larger impact on the team and the business. As such, the weight attached to your decision-making and responsibilities increases. For technical roles like portfolio management or trading, you'll be expected to have a larger impact and more meaningful contribution to the team's revenue numbers. And for non-technical roles like sales, you'll also be expected to make a greater contribution to the team's revenue figures, by expanding your existing client base.

At this level you'll be overseeing deal execution, coordinating across divisions, taking clients out to events, and working closely with directors and managing directors. They'll be the ones setting the tone and goals for the team, and you'll be tasked with ensuring that all objectives are met by utilising the resources of the team (i.e. analysts and associates) in as effective a way as possible.

The vice president/executive director role is all about results delivery, managing complex projects, and further developing client relationships. Once you're comfortable doing so, and you're consistently bringing in new business, you'll be up for a director-level promotion within a year or two. However, at this level of the corporate ladder it really does become more about results and showing your work, in order to prove you're capable and deserving of the next promotion. It's a demanding role that tests your ability to lead, become extremely commercial by bringing in new business, and also take on a mentor-type role guiding analysts and associates in their careers. All of this is considered before you're promoted to director level.

Keep in mind, some firms don't split the vice president/executive director and director roles. They consider them all the same. So instead of having to go from associate to vice president/executive director, to director, and then to managing director, you can go from associate to vice president/executive director/director to managing director. Therefore, moving from associate to managing director takes two promotions instead of three at some firms.

DIRECTOR

Directors, often interchangeable with the vice president/executive director role at some firms, sit just below the managing director role. These individuals are essentially seasoned vice presidents/executive directors and on track to reach the managing director position. They've established their presence in the team and division and consistently contribute in a meaningful way to the business, whether it be through a solid investing or trading track record, bringing in new business through clients, or executing exciting and meaningful deals.

Directors are also expected to work with managing directors in order to assess, review, and set the team's business strategy moving forward. As such, you'll be expected to have a solid understanding and awareness of the industry, a strong client network, and the ability to think strategically about new market opportunities.

The responsibilities that come with this role, and accommodate a large pay package, often require you to pitch new business, manage high-stakes client relationships, and lead large teams. If the team is struggling or not performing as expected, the managing director will be coming to you for answers. So taking on the role of director comes with a plethora of high expectations and increased pressure from senior management.

MANAGING DIRECTOR

The managing director position is often the highest rank at most firms. It's the pinnacle of the industry and where true finance and banking die-hards aim to be before retiring. The truth is, being promoted to the managing director position isn't guaranteed. Unlike the positions before reaching the managing director title, only a handful of vice presidents/executive directors and directors will ever make it to the managing director level. A few reasons for this include the fact that it's an extremely results-oriented role. You truly have to love the work and be exceptional. Most people who reach the vice president/executive director or director position are more than happy to stay in such a position, earn a very comfortable living, and do so without killing themselves with the added pressure and expectations that come with being a managing director. In truth, most people simply aren't cut out to be managing directors. It's a greatly coveted position, but one that carries a lot of weight.

In contrast, if you manage to climb to the managing director level you'll enjoy a huge pay package that consists of cash and equity, as well as bonuses that reflect the team's, division's, and firm's performance for the year. The total compensation at this level can range from the multi-hundreds of thousands to multi-millions of dollars depending on your role and division. For example, managing directors who are working in the front office and are directly responsible for generating revenue through trading, executing deals, or managing portfolios will earn substantially more in base salaries and bonuses than managing directors working in middle or back-office functions that aren't generating revenue.

To succeed as a managing director, you'll need to have strong internal and external connections and networks, be well respected by your peers and colleagues, have a solid grasp of the commercial side of the business, regularly innovate from a strategic standpoint, have the ability to manage complex client relationships, and manage a range of different personalities and individuals within your team. You'll also need to be someone who people like working for, as you'll be responsible for setting the culture across the team.

In terms of the timeline to get promoted to managing director, it's tricky to give an estimate since it varies from person to person. Unlike most other roles where you'll likely be promoted if you spend a certain number of years in the role and aren't extremely terrible at performing it, this isn't the case for becoming a managing director. I've seen people at Goldman Sachs promoted to managing director at the age of 27. This is rare, but it happens when firms realise they have an extremely talented individual and don't want to lose them to a competitor. As such, they'll promote the individual faster than usual, offer a substantial compensation and benefits package, and hope they stay at the firm. If I had to take a guess, I'd say most people who get promoted to managing director do so within 10–15 years; however, for others it can take 20 years or longer.

The only way to guarantee that you reach the managing director level, if that's what you truly want, is to simply be exceptional at your job. It might cost you a healthy work–life balance, grey your hair sooner than you'd like, prematurely age you (given the years of stress), and mean missing important family events, but if it's what you truly want, I do think that the industry is a meritocracy that provides opportunities for the most capable individuals with a proven track record.

PARTNER

Being a partner is the most prestigious title in the industry. This role exists in very few investment banks, Goldman Sachs being one of them, and is only reserved for the cream of the crop (i.e. the handful of managing directors who are too important for the firm to lose). The individuals that reach partner status are world class at what they do and are the most senior, highest-performing individuals who have demonstrated exceptional business impact.

One of the most common ways in which partners differ from managing directors is that the managing director is usually responsible for a team within a division; however, the partner is likely to play a part in the strategic decision-making and direction that impacts multiple teams or an entire division. They also hold an ownership stake in the firm and so their compensation package is easily in the millions of dollars.

On a day-to-day basis, partners bring in large, high-profile clients or deals, have unparalleled client networks, and set the tone for the division's and/or firm's culture and direction. These individuals are accountable for the division's and/or firm's performance and success and are often involved in key decision-making at the board level.

Reaching partner status is a seriously impressive and immense achievement, which reflects years of dedication to the industry, high performance, and significant contributions to the firm's success.

CHAPTER 7

SALARIES AND COMPENSATION

It's no mystery that the earning potential in the world of banking and finance careers is extremely lucrative and one of the factors that drive so many ambitious and bright graduates into the field each year. It's true that at the pinnacle of a career in this world you can take home millions of dollars in salary, bonuses, and stock options. And yes, the base salaries reach six figures faster than most other industries. However, remember that this is a results-driven industry, where performance and revenue generation are paramount. This means you'll be paid handsomely if you're bringing in money for the firm; however, if you're having a tough year, or the business has recently been hit with a huge fine, or the global financial markets are experiencing a tough time in the economic cycle, it'll be reflected in your year-end bonus. There'll be good years and there'll be bad years, but if you're consistently not performing as expected, you'll be at risk of being fired.

As with all roles and industries, finance and banking salaries will always vary from firm to firm, team to team, and division to division.

Front-office, revenue-generating roles will typically pay more than back-office, non-revenue-generating roles; analysts in the same division will earn lower base salaries than associates in the same division and the same is true for associates to vice presidents/executive directors, and so on up the corporate career ladder. However, it's not uncommon for an analyst in a front-office division to earn more than an associate in a back-office division.

Two other factors worth considering include the region and the type of firm. For example, New York tends to pay higher salaries than London, and elite boutiques and niche hedge funds are often able to pay higher total compensation packages to their bankers and traders compared to bulge bracket investment banks given the nature of their business, client or sector focus, small company size, and so on.

Here's a breakdown of typical salary ranges for front- and back-office roles, from analyst to managing director, in both London and New York. This data comes from sources like Mergers & Inquisitions, eFinancial-Careers, Glassdoor, and Payscale.

In front-office roles within investment banking in London, analysts can expect a base salary between £60,000 and £90,000, with total compensation reaching around £100,000–£150,000. As analysts progress up the ladder to the associate level, the base salary jumps to £100,000–£125,000, with total compensation typically between £140,000 and £190,000. Vice presidents and executive directors see a further boost, with base salaries from £150,000 to £165,000 and total compensation between £250,000 and £300,000. Next, we have directors or senior vice presidents, for whom the base salary is around £178,000 and total compensation averages around £333,000. Last but not least, at the managing director level one can expect a base salary of around £243,000 and total compensation between £319,000 and £509,000. These figures reflect both the responsibility and the revenue-generating expectations placed on front-office roles and will vary hugely based on individual performance and many other factors.

In New York, front-office salaries are typically higher (keep in mind the cost of living is generally more expensive in New York than London), with analysts earning base salaries between $100,000 and $125,000, pushing total compensation to around $140,000–$190,000. Associates see a substantial increase, with base salary ranging from $175,000 to $225,000 and total pay between $225,000 and $425,000. Vice presidents/executive directors command base salaries from $250,000 to $300,000, and total compensation can range from $450,000 to $650,000. At the director or senior vice president level, base salaries are between $300,000 and $350,000, while total compensation can reach $550,000–$750,000. And for managing directors, as expected, the numbers are even higher, with base pay between $400,000 and $600,000 and total earnings from $600,000 to well over $1 million.

In back-office roles like operations and compliance, and middle-office roles like risk management, salaries are comparatively lower but still competitive.

In London, entry-level analysts can expect a base salary of £35,000–£50,000, with total compensation between £40,000 and £60,000. Associates earn a base salary of around £50,000–£70,000 and total compensation ranges from £60,000 to £85,000. Vice presidents/executive directors earn between £70,000 and £100,000 in base salary, with total earnings between £85,000 and £120,000. Directors or senior vice presidents earn a base of £100,000–£130,000, with total pay in the range of £120,000–£160,000, while managing directors in the back office generally see base salaries from £130,000 to £180,000 and total compensation around £160,000–£220,000.

In New York, like the front office, back-office roles follow a similar structure but with slightly higher numbers. Analysts in these roles have base salaries between $60,000 and $80,000, bringing total compensation to $70,000–$90,000. Associates earn a base of around $80,000–$110,000, and total compensation ranges from $90,000 to $130,000. Vice president/executive director roles offer base salaries from $110,000 to $150,000 and total compensation can reach $130,000–$180,000. For directors or senior vice presidents, base pay is between $150,000 and $200,000, with total compensation around $180,000–$240,000. Managing directors in the back office earn between $200,000 and $250,000 in base salary, with total compensation between $240,000 and $300,000.

These figures should provide a general guideline, but as previously mentioned, exact compensation will depend on the firm, individual performance, and market conditions, among other factors.

CHAPTER 8

PROS AND CONS OF A CAREER IN FINANCE AND BANKING

REASONS FOR BUILDING A CAREER IN THIS INDUSTRY

A career in the world of finance and banking is more than just a job. It's often considered a gateway to a world of opportunities, challenges, and rewards that few other industries can offer. Whether you're drawn to the excitement of financial markets, the intellectual challenge of problem-solving, or the allure of competitive compensation, there are countless reasons why this industry continues to attract ambitious individuals. Let's go through a few of the most common reasons.

Endless Opportunities for Growth

One of the biggest positives of working in finance and banking is the sheer variety of opportunities available across all seniority and experience levels. The industry offers a range of roles, from investment banking and asset management to technology and compliance. As your career progresses, you can either specialise in a specific area, switch divisions, or even move into entirely new regions. Most roles in this industry are globally focused, meaning your skills are transferable and in demand across countries. This offers the exciting opportunity to build an international career if that's something you're interested in. To add to that, the industry thrives on meritocracy, so if you're driven, talented, and consistently able to deliver results, the opportunities to progress are endless. Firms would rather promote and keep you, as opposed to losing you to a competitor.

Financial Rewards

It's no secret that finance and banking are among the most lucrative industries, especially for graduates considering the prospect of earning up to $100,000 starting salaries straight out of the gate. Competitive salaries, performance bonuses, and long-term incentives like stock options or carried interest (performance-related rewards) are the norm in this industry. For example, the culprits most commonly known to earn big bucks are the investment bankers and private equity professionals, who often enjoy salaries and bonuses that far outpace those in other industries. But it's not just the top-tier roles that pay handsomely. Most mid-level positions, and even junior roles across the industry, can come with compensation packages that provide comfortable financial security and stability from the outset.

Intellectual Stimulation

For those who thrive on solving complex problems, few industries are as mentally stimulating as finance and banking. Whether you're structuring multi-million-dollar deals, analysing investment opportunities, or investing across global markets, the work in each division challenges you to think critically, act decisively, and adapt quickly. Yes, some divisions are more intellectually stimulating than others; however, for the most part, each day typically comes with its own set of challenges and learning opportunities, and the ever-changing nature of the industry ensures you're constantly learning. As such, this intellectual rigour not only sharpens your skills but also keeps the job exciting.

Building a Valuable Skill Set

A career in finance equips you with skills that are highly transferable and sought after across many other industries. Whether it's financial modelling and data analysis or negotiation and strategic thinking, the tools you develop in finance are universally applicable. And it's not just the hard, technical skills I'm talking about. Working in this industry, especially in a front-office role, for example, will equip you with an elite range of soft skills that can be applied across industries, roles, and businesses. As a result, these skills can open doors beyond banking, allowing you to pivot into other sectors like consulting, technology, or even entrepreneurship. In saying this, it's no surprise that many successful founders and politicians started their careers in finance, leveraging the knowledge, interpersonal skills, work ethic, and networks they built along the way.

Networking and Prestige

Working in finance and banking often means interacting with high-profile clients, senior executives, CEOs, and other industry leaders. These relationships not only expand your network but can also open doors to exciting opportunities for your career in the future. Additionally, the prestige associated with working at a top-tier firm like Goldman Sachs, J.P. Morgan, or Morgan Stanley can significantly enhance your personal brand and credibility, both within and outside the industry.

A Front-Row Seat to Global Events

Finance professionals are at the heart of global economic activity. You're not just observing market trends. You're actively shaping them. From advising companies on mergers and acquisitions, to connecting multi-billion-dollar buyers and sellers, and investing the capital that shapes the future retirement prospects of workforces all over the world, your work has a direct impact on industries and economies globally. This exposure gives you a unique perspective on global affairs and a sense of purpose that can go beyond personal achievement.

Personal Development

When you enter the world of finance and banking, some divisions will make you feel like a fish out of water. You'll be thrown in the deep end to see if you sink or swim. This is a good thing. It means you're being given an opportunity to step outside of your comfort zone in order to develop and grow. The fast-paced environment, high-pressure situations, and need for precision develop qualities like resilience, attention to detail, and confidence. These aren't just career-enhancing skills but life skills that'll benefit you outside of your career.

Summary

To sum up, a career in finance and banking isn't just about earning a high salary or working for a prestigious firm. It's about the opportunities to grow, learn, and make a tangible impact on the world around you. For those willing to put in the hard work, the professional and personal rewards are extremely attractive. If you're someone who thrives under pressure, enjoys constantly being in work mode, finds joy in solving problems, and has big ambitions, the world of finance and banking could be the right place for you to start your career.

THE DOWNSIDE OF A CAREER IN THIS INDUSTRY

We've covered the major positives for considering building your career in the world of finance and banking; however, it's only fair that I bring you back to reality by covering some of the most common challenges that individuals in this industry face. These include high-pressure working environments, long hours, extremely competitive cultures, intense workloads, stress, poor work–life balance, and more. The frequency and magnitude of these challenges can make it a difficult career path for most. This is why it's important to understand the potential downsides before committing to a role in the demanding world of finance and banking.

Long Hours and Intense Workloads

One of the most talked-about drawbacks of finance and banking is the gruelling schedule. For front-office roles like investment banking or private equity, working 80–100 hours a week is common. Late nights, early mornings, and weekend work are often the norm, especially during deal cycles or earnings seasons. While some divisions, like asset management or middle-office roles, might offer a little more balance, the intensity is still higher than in many other industries. As a result, this can take a significant toll on your personal life, making it difficult to maintain relationships or pursue hobbies.

Stress and High Pressure

This industry isn't for the faint-hearted. The stakes are high, whether you're managing millions in client assets, advising on billion-dollar deals, or market-making. The pressure to perform can be relentless, with expectations to meet tight deadlines and deliver exceptional results, or potentially lose out on your end-of-year bonus, or even worse, be fired. Some people thrive in such high-pressure environments; however, for most, it can lead to burnout, anxiety, or other mental health challenges.

Cutthroat Competition

Finance is one of the most competitive industries in the world. From the moment you start applying for spring weeks, internships, or graduate schemes, you're competing against the brightest and most ambitious candidates. Once inside, the competition doesn't stop. Promotions, bonuses, and even job security can depend on your ability to outperform your peers. Annual rankings are common at many firms and used to determine promotions and bonuses. For those who thrive on collaboration rather than competition, some divisions (sales and trading) might feel overly aggressive and draining compared to others (asset management).

Limited Work–Life Balance

Achieving a healthy work–life balance in finance can feel nearly impossible, especially in your early years. Junior professionals, like analysts or associates, often sacrifice their personal time to meet work demands. And I think that's okay early on in your career, especially if you've not started your own family yet and don't have too many responsibilities outside of work. However, as time goes on and you get older, work–life balance will increase in importance. As a result, interrupted holidays and weekends, and constantly being 'on call' (which is common in some roles), will prove less and less appealing. While the industry rewards hard work, this imbalance can lead to dissatisfaction and a sense of missing out on important personal milestones.

Repetitive and Transactional Work

Although finance is often portrayed as glamorous, with each day offering new and exciting opportunities, the reality is that many roles involve repetitive tasks, particularly in the early stages of your career. Building financial models, preparing pitch decks, settling trades, or reconciling data can feel monotonous after a while. The transactional nature of some roles, especially in investment banking, can leave you feeling disconnected from the broader purpose of your work. After all, at the junior levels your main responsibility is to take care of the grunt work, to a high standard.

Cyclical Job Security

The world of finance and banking is heavily influenced by the global financial markets. As such, economic downturns, regulatory changes, geopolitics, or shifts in client demand can lead to layoffs or hiring freezes. Even high performers can find themselves at risk of being made redundant during restructuring or cost-cutting initiatives. This lack of job security, particularly in front-office roles where salaries are highest, adds an element of unpredictability to any finance career.

Mental and Physical Health

When you decide to work in this industry, it's worth knowing that you'll be required to make a sacrifice somewhere in your life. Since you'll have limited free time, you'll have to constantly decide between spending time with friends and family, going to the gym, having some of your own downtime, and sleeping. To add to that, if you're working long hours, constantly on call, and not prioritising healthy lifestyle habits, chances are you'll add a few pounds to the waistline as the months and years pass by. I can't lie, this kind of happened to me during my time in the city. And it's not just a physical health concern that's the issue. The demanding nature of this industry can take a toll on both mental and physical health. Sleep deprivation, poor diet, and lack of exercise are common issues for those working long hours. By the time you're done working, you're likely too exhausted to even think about going to the gym, even if it's just downstairs (most bulge bracket investment banks have everything you need to keep you within those four walls, from a health centre with a gym to an in-house doctor, a nursery for employees' children, and more).

Even though I was in the asset management division, which is considered less intense than other front-office divisions such as the trading floor or investment banking, I witnessed a colleague experience a series of heart-related issues which kept them out of work for a while, whilst another was experiencing serious depression. Whether these were work related or not, it wouldn't surprise me if the intensity, never-ending to-do lists, and pressure to always perform at 100% played a role. This is why it's important to prioritise self-care if you ever find yourself heading down the road to burnout.

High Barriers to Entry

Breaking into finance and banking is notoriously difficult. As much as the industry is getting better at recruiting from more universities, there's definitely still a heavy bias towards candidates from elite target universities. This exists because a lot of professionals already in the industry went to elite schools and so have a natural bias towards those who share some form of mutual affiliation. Having said this, what holds a lot of weight in applications is being able to show you have relevant internships or experience. The truth is, without these credentials, the path becomes even more challenging. After all, you'll be competing with candidates who have spring weeks, internships (sometimes more than one), and so on. For those who do break in, the pressure to continually prove yourself in order to earn the large salary and bonus can feel quite overwhelming.

Summary

Building a career in the world of finance and banking comes with undeniable rewards, but just like any good thing, it's not without its sacrifices. The long hours, intense pressure, and competitive culture can take a toll on even the most driven individuals. If you're considering this path, it's crucial to weigh the pros and cons, understand what you're getting into, and decide whether the challenges align with your goals and personality. Don't get me wrong, it's a solid industry to break into, learn a ton of attractive skills, and leave with exciting exit opportunities. For those of you who thrive under pressure and are prepared to make the sacrifices, the rewards can be immense. But do keep in mind, it's not for everyone.

CHAPTER 9

PRIVATE EQUITY, HEDGE FUNDS, AND VENTURE CAPITAL

PRIVATE EQUITY

Private equity is one of the most sought-after and lucrative areas of finance. At its core, it is about investing in companies, either private businesses or public firms that have been taken private, with the goal of enhancing their value and eventually selling them at a significant profit. The difference between public market investors (those who buy and sell stocks and shares through a public stock exchange) and private equity professionals is that public market investors invest with minimal interaction, whereas private equity professionals dive deep into the businesses they acquire, taking a hands-on approach to strategy, operations, and management.

Private equity firms pool capital from institutional investors like pension funds, sovereign wealth funds, and endowments to create investment funds. These funds can range in size from hundreds of millions to billions of dollars. Once a fund has reached its target size (e.g. the private equity firm has leveraged its connections and clients to pool the capital together), these funds are then used to buy companies, improve them, and eventually exit at a higher valuation. The ultimate goal here is to create value and deliver strong returns for investors.

An important concept to understand is that of illiquidity. When we say an asset or investment is liquid, it basically means it's pretty easy to turn that asset or investment into cash. On the other hand, when something is illiquid, it means it'll take longer to turn that asset or investment into cash. As such, private equity investments are considered illiquid since firms hold onto their investments for several years (anywhere from 5 to 15 years) before being able to make an exit and generate a return for everyone that's invested in the fund. This long-term horizon gives private equity firms the time they need to implement transformative changes, restructure businesses, and drive operational improvements.

Common Private Equity Strategies

Private equity firms don't just buy companies, they also focus on strategies that add value and drive growth. Some of the most common strategies include:

- leveraged buyouts
- growth equity
- distressed investing

- venture capital
- secondaries

Let's go through these one by one.

Leveraged buyouts (LBOs) are the bread and butter of private equity investing and typically involve acquiring a company using a mix of equity and debt, where the debt is repaid using the company's future cash flows. The goal here is to improve the company's operations and profitability, so that it can be sold at a higher valuation and generate strong returns.

Growth equity focuses on investing in established companies that need funding in order to expand into new markets, launch products, or scale their operations. Unlike LBOs, growth equity typically involves less debt and more of a partnership approach.

Distressed investing, also known as turnaround investing, is a strategy that targets companies in financial trouble. Private equity firms target these struggling businesses, acquire them, stabilise their operations, restructure their debt, and return them to profitability before making an exit.

Venture capital is technically a subset of private equity and focuses on startups and early-stage companies. At its core, venture capital is all about funding innovation and investing in high-risk, high-growth potential startups (which we'll cover in more detail shortly).

Secondaries involve buying stakes in existing private equity funds or portfolios from other investors. Secondaries offer diversification and liquidity to investors who are interested in exiting their private equity investments early.

The Private Equity Deal Cycle

Private equity investments typically follow a well-defined cycle, which includes fundraising, sourcing deals, due diligence, acquisition, and, last but not least, portfolio management.

At the fundraising stage, private equity firms raise capital from institutional investors, promising to deploy that capital over a specific time frame. These investors, called limited partners (LPs), trust the private equity firm, the general partner (GP), to generate returns.

Once the GP has raised enough capital from its clients, they'll close the fund to any new capital and start focusing on deal sourcing. This is where they're trying to identify potential investment opportunities to use the capital they've raised to invest in. This is also where the power of networking, market research, and existing connections and relationships with investment banks come into play.

After the firm has sourced attractive deals, they'll shift their focus to due diligence, which is another term for carrying out in-depth research and background checks or investigations on a business. There'll be an operational due diligence team within the firm that conducts extensive due diligence, evaluating financial performance, operational risks, and growth potential. Once they've carried out their investigations and reviews, they'll feed it all back to the investors and key decision-makers to decide whether to move forward with an acquisition or not.

Once a deal is approved, the private equity firm negotiates terms in order to acquire the company, often using significant leverage (debt). This goes back to the most common strategy in private equity (i.e. LBOs).

Next, the real work begins. The portfolio management team collaborates with the company in order to implement operational changes (sometimes this means firing tons of employees and it is often the reason why private equity investors have a bad reputation), improve profitability, and prepare for a lucrative exit. The process of turning around a business doesn't happen overnight. In fact, it can take many years.

After several years, the firm sells its stake in the company, typically through a trade sale (acquisition of one company by another), initial public offering (IPO), or secondary sale (one private equity firm buys the investment or stake in the company from another private equity firm). A successful exit is how private equity firms generate their returns and are able to pay their employees hundreds of thousands to multi-millions of dollars in compensation and bonuses each year.

Why Private Equity Is So Attractive

Private equity is often seen as the end goal when it comes to finance and banking careers. Most graduates who land in investment banking aim to work there for two to three years before making the move over to private equity. Private equity firms are able to attract top-tier talent because the industry offers more than just high compensation. The work is intellectually stimulating, combining financial analysis, operational problem-solving, and strategic thinking. In investment banking you're mostly working on financial modelling, creating presentations, and advising companies, and although you'll still be doing a lot of this in private equity, you'll also be introduced to more interesting responsibilities like investing in and turning around businesses. For many, the real appeal lies in the combination of making an impact, a better work–life balance, turning around struggling businesses, creating growth, and earning lucrative pay packages.

It's worth noting an important differentiator in pay for private equity professionals. Beyond base salaries and bonuses, private equity professionals also earn carried interest, which is a share of the profits from successful deals. This performance-based structure aligns incentives and rewards success. So the larger the deals that are successfully executed, the larger the take-home pay for the employees who worked on such deals. This differs from the investment banking business where you charge a fee for advising on a transaction or acquisition, as opposed to being able to participate and take a share of any profits.

Summary

Private equity is about more than just buying and selling companies. It's about creating value, driving growth, and transforming businesses. For those who enjoy strategic thinking, financial analysis, and making a tangible impact, private equity offers a challenging and rewarding career path. Whether you're interested in helping a struggling company find its footing or scaling a business to new heights, private equity could be a career worth considering.

HEDGE FUNDS

Hedge funds are one of the most intriguing, opaque, and fast-paced areas in finance, offering a unique combination of flexibility, innovation, and the potential for outsized returns. These firms, or investment vehicles, are designed to cater to clients who are willing to take on higher risks in search of greater rewards. As such, hedge funds not only attract top talent with the promise of high earnings but also with the intellectual challenge of working on complex strategies in ever-changing markets. In this section I'll go over what they are, how they operate, common hedge fund investment strategies, clients, and roles. With that, let's kick off with a very common question: What exactly is a hedge fund?

At their core, hedge funds are pooled investment vehicles that manage money for high-net-worth individuals, institutional investors, and accredited investors (wealthy individuals who meet certain regulatory criteria). Unlike traditional investment funds like mutual funds, hedge funds are far less regulated. As a result, this reduced oversight gives them the flexibility to invest in a wide variety of assets and employ advanced strategies that more traditional funds aren't allowed to.

While we're on the topic of hedge funds, it's worth defining the term. To 'hedge' means simply to protect, or reduce the risk against something happening. Hedge funds primarily aim to minimise risk, but at the same time many aim to generate excessive returns by taking calculated risks through innovative and aggressive investment strategies.

Key Strategies

Hedge funds are as varied as the markets they operate in, and their success often comes down to the strategies they employ. Most hedge funds tend to have a very narrow focus on a specific strategy or sector of the industry. Having said this, some do indeed have a slightly broader approach to investing. As you can imagine, each type of strategy comes with its own strengths and weaknesses.

Some of the most popular hedge fund strategies include:

- long/short equity
- global macro
- event-driven
- market-neutral
- quantitative
- distressed investing

Let's go through each of these individually.

Long/short equity is one of the most common hedge fund strategies, which involves buying undervalued stocks (long positions) and shorting overvalued ones. By doing this, the fund can profit (in theory) irrespective of whether markets rise or fall, as gains from short positions offset losses from longs during downturns.

Global macro funds focus on taking advantage of macroeconomic trends, making large bets on factors like currency movements, interest rate changes, or geopolitical news. Global macro hedge fund managers use economic data and global trends to forecast such market shifts.

Event-driven hedge funds capitalise on opportunities created by corporate events, such as mergers, acquisitions, bankruptcies, or restructurings. For example, when two companies merge, or one company is acquired by another, the typical outcome is an increase in the share prices of these companies. As such, these hedge fund managers aim to invest in these companies in order to benefit from the eventual completion of a merger, or the recovery of a company undergoing restructuring.

Market-neutral hedge funds focus on eliminating the exposure to overall market movements by balancing long and short positions. The focus here is purely on the performance of individual stocks or sectors rather than broader market trends.

Quantitative (quant) funds rely on mathematical models and algorithms to identify trading opportunities. These strategies are heavily data-driven and often executed at high speeds across multiple markets. The advantage of finding such opportunities and executing them before other players across the financial markets can be worth billions for these hedge funds.

Distressed investing funds target companies which are struggling financially. They buy the debt from these companies (or the equity) at a heavy discount. The end goal here is to profit when the company recovers, either through restructuring or an operational turnaround.

It's not uncommon for hedge fund managers to get creative and combine a mixture of these strategies, or develop their own proprietary methods in order to capitalise on unique opportunities in the market. As such, these inventive strategies make the hedge fund industry one of the most innovative and exciting places to build a career.

Clients

Hedge funds cater to investors with significant capital to invest and a high tolerance for risk. Typical clients, similar to private equity and asset management clients, include, but are not limited to, high-net-worth individuals, institutional investors (pension funds, endowments, insurance companies, governments, corporates, etc.), family offices (investment firms managing the wealth of affluent families), and funds of funds (funds that invest in multiple hedge funds to achieve broader diversification).

These investors are happy to invest a portion of their capital towards illiquid investments and are particularly drawn to hedge funds for their potential to deliver high returns and provide portfolio diversification, especially during times of market volatility.

Roles

Working in a hedge fund is challenging, competitive, and rewarding. On top of that, it's no easy feat breaking into a hedge fund. However, if you're keen on exploring careers in this space it's worth knowing about the different roles most hedge funds have on offer. These include:

- research analysts
- traders
- portfolio managers
- quantitative researchers and developers
- risk managers
- operation and compliance specialists

Research analysts dive deep into financial data, sectors, or markets to generate actionable investment ideas. These individuals are responsible for building financial models, conducting research, and presenting insights to portfolio managers.

Traders are responsible for executing the strategies designed by portfolio managers. They need a solid understanding of market mechanics and have to act quickly in order to take advantage of unique opportunities that arise in the market.

Portfolio managers, typically the highest earners at funds, oversee funds or specific strategies, make investment decisions, and bear ultimate responsibility for the specific fund's or strategy's performance. They combine research, risk management, and strategy execution in order to meet the return targets that the fund sets out to achieve.

Quantitative researchers and developers work on developing the mathematical models and algorithms that drive quantitative strategies. These roles require expertise in programming, mathematics, and statistical analysis. If you're interested in this type of career you'll typically need a highly technical academic background, often at PhD level.

Risk managers ensure that the fund's strategies align with its risk appetite. They monitor exposures, assess potential losses, and use advanced tools to minimise risk. They're essentially safeguarding any major losses and keeping an eye on the decisions that portfolio managers and traders are making.

Operations and compliance specialists handle the back-office work, ensuring trades settle smoothly, accounts are reconciled, and regulatory requirements are met. Yes, every firm has a back office which is oftentimes forgotten by students and graduates. Working in a back-office role is also an easy way to get your foot in the door of highly competitive and prestigious firms like hedge funds—which is always worth considering if you're struggling to land those intense, competitive, and extremely popular front-office roles.

As with all firms across the world of finance, hedge funds are performance-driven, so progression often depends on delivering results. As such, top performers are able to rise quickly and unlock substantial rewards.

Summary

Hedge funds are about more than just big bets. They're about innovation, strategy, and navigating complex markets. For those who thrive in high-pressure environments and enjoy solving challenging problems, hedge funds offer a career that's both rewarding and intellectually stimulating. Whether you're drawn by the potential for high earnings or the chance to make an impact on global markets, hedge funds represent the cutting edge of the financial world. They're not easy to break into, and they come with a lot of pressure and stress, but if these are things you're willing to put up with, succeeding in this industry can be extremely worthwhile.

VENTURE CAPITAL

Of the three 'alternative' career paths (private equity, hedge funds, and venture capital), my personal favourite is venture capital. It's one of the most exciting and influential areas in finance, playing a pivotal role in backing the ideas and technologies that will likely define the world of tomorrow. This industry is a branch of private equity that focuses exclusively on startups and early-stage companies, providing them with the capital and support they need to grow.

Venture capital investing is the ultimate type of investing when it comes to high risk. Venture capital firms are essentially betting on small teams to innovate and grow with the hope of reaping rewards that are 100 to 1,000 times bigger than their initial investment. They place bets on tons of different companies with the hope that at least one of those companies will return the entire portfolio (i.e. return more than all the others combined). These businesses often have groundbreaking ideas or disruptive technologies but lack the funding to scale. And this is where venture capitalists step in, offering capital in exchange for equity (ownership) in the company.

This isn't a safe bet, far from it. After all, most startups fail, and venture capitalists know they're taking on a significant level of risk. But when it works, it works big. Companies like Google, Facebook, and Amazon all benefited from venture capital early on, and the returns for their investors were astronomical. For example, Peter Thiel, a highly respected entrepreneur, investor, and former CEO of PayPal, invested $500,000 in Facebook in 2004 and sold shares worth over $1 billion when Facebook went public in 2012. That's almost a 200,000% return. In contrast, you'll be lucky to get an annual return of 20% investing in an S&P 500 index.

Stages of Venture Capital Investing

Venture capital funding doesn't come in one lump sum, it's broken into stages, with each phase aligned to the startup's growth.

The earliest funding phase is called the *seed* stage, often used to turn an idea into a prototype or product. At this stage, companies typically raise anywhere from a few hundred thousand dollars to a million or two million dollars. The focus here is on market research, hiring, or building the foundation of the business. It's a high-risk stage, as the company is often just starting.

Next, we have the *series A* stage. At this point, the product or service is usually developed, and the focus shifts to refining the business model and scaling operations. Series A funding rounds can range from a few million dollars up to the tens or twenties of millions of dollars, and help grow the customer base, expand the team, and develop marketing strategies.

Following a series A will be a *series B*, *series C*, and so on. These rounds aim to take the company to the next level, whether that's scaling further, entering new markets, or launching additional products. The size of these rounds will vary, but it's not uncommon for them to be in the $30–40 million range, all the way up to and exceeding $100 million dollars. When the investment rounds reach these levels, they typically end up attracting institutional investors.

Finally, we have an *exit*. This is when venture capitalists cash out. An exit could come through an IPO or a sale to another company. This is the ultimate goal for investors, as it means the potential for substantial returns after many years.

How Venture Capital Firms Work

Similar to private equity firms and hedge funds, venture capital firms raise money from institutional investors, high-net-worth individuals, and family offices. Similar to established private equity funds, these clients, known as LPs, pool their funds into a venture capital fund, which is managed by the venture capitalist or GP. The venture capital firm then invests this money into a portfolio of startups, aiming to spread risk across multiple bets.

But venture capital firms don't just bring money to the table. They actively support their portfolio companies by providing strategic advice, mentorship, and access to an extensive network. This hands-on involvement is often crucial in helping startups navigate challenges and scale successfully.

Roles in Venture Capital

Venture capital firms run lean operations, but they offer a variety of roles that require a mix of analytical skills, relationship-building, and strategic thinking. If you're ever considering breaking into this industry, it's worth knowing about the roles that they offer, which include:

- analyst
- associate
- principal
- partner

Analysts, who are entry level, focus on market research, evaluating potential investments, and building financial models. They support the deal team by identifying opportunities and conducting due diligence.

Associates take on a more active role in deal execution, working directly with founders and portfolio companies. This position requires a balance of technical ability and interpersonal skills.

Principals are senior team members who source deals, negotiate terms, and oversee investments. They bridge the gap between associates and partners.

Partners lead the firm's strategy, manage LP relationships, and make final investment decisions. They're also deeply involved in mentoring startups and ensuring the success of the portfolio.

As with all firms in the world of finance and banking, the higher up you climb in the venture capital world, the more responsibilities you'll take on board, and the better compensation packages you'll unlock.

Is Venture Capital for You?

A career in venture capital is perfect for those who thrive on innovation, strategy, and helping businesses succeed. It's a high-risk, high-reward environment that demands strong analytical skills, business acumen, and relationship management. People often break into venture capital from investment banking given their ability to create financial models and experience in valuing companies (even though venture capital firms deal with companies that are practically impossible to value given how early on in their journey they are). Whether you're drawn by the chance to back the next Facebook or AirBnB, or to be at the forefront of solving global challenges, venture capital offers a unique and fulfilling career path.

PART II
BREAKING IN

CHAPTER 10

THE APPLICATION PROCESS

Anyone and everyone who wants to break into the industry will face at least one, if not most, of the hurdles in the application process that I'll cover in this chapter. The stages of the application process typically include, but are not limited to, the following:

- submission of personal and academic details
- CV upload
- cover letter upload
- motivational questions
- psychometric tests
- online interviews
- telephone interviews
- in-person interviews
- assessment centres

This application process has been around for a long time and many view parts of it as outdated for the current world we live in. With the growth of technology, artificial intelligence, and a move away from traditional selection criteria such as CV and cover letter uploads by companies outside the world of finance and banking, I wouldn't be surprised if finance and banking firms start doing the same. However, for now, this isn't the case and so it's important to be aware of what's expected in these areas for any applications you submit.

In terms of time frame, the entire process from preparing and submitting an application to going through the selection process of assessment centres and interviews to successfully securing an offer typically takes months and consists of two parts:

1. *Application prep.* Maximise your chances of securing interviews by creating a compelling CV, cover letter, and so on. Without a strong application submission you stand no chance of being invited for interviews, assessment centres, or even the next stage of the online application process, which is often being requested to undertake a range of online psychometric tests. Preparing your application for success will take weeks to months and is an ongoing process that you'll keep improving and iterating on. The more applications you do, the better your future application submissions become as you learn and improve from each rejection or acceptance response from firms. As long as you try and improve one thing from application to application you'll be proceeding successfully in no time.

2. *Selection process.* The second part is where things begin to feel a little more real. It's when your initial application has been successful and you've been invited to go through the selection process by attending an assessment centre and interviews. Going through the selection process is highly demanding and competitive (since you're now

competing with the best candidates from thousands of applications). Some firms are better than others at letting you know as soon as possible if you've been successful or not. This part of the selection process can take anywhere from a few weeks to a month or so. However, mastering assessment centres and interviews can often take a lot longer.

Over the next few pages I'll break down in more detail what each stage of the application and selection process entails. They'll also be covered in greater detail in their own respective sections later on in the book, explaining how best to approach and prepare for them.

CV/RÉSUMÉ

The CV (otherwise known as a résumé) is arguably the most important one-page document you'll ever write before leaving the world of academia and entering the world of work. It's a one-page document created to pitch you to the reader (i.e. the employee or HR professional at any company you apply to). It does this by highlighting your academic and work experiences to date, focusing particularly on important and relevant key skills and competencies that you've developed over time.

COVER LETTER

The cover letter is essentially a one-page document where you're explaining why you're interested in the organisation and the role and why you think you're the most suitable candidate that they should consider. The job of the cover letter is to build enough curiosity in the reader about you to want to find out more and thus invite you in for an interview or assessment centre.

We typically follow a three-part structure for cover letters, which includes answering the following:

- Why are you interested in this company?
- Why are you interested in this division?
- Why should they hire you specifically?

MOTIVATIONAL QUESTIONS

Many applications you submit for investment banks and other financial institutions will require you to answer a number of motivational questions. These questions aim to identify your reasons and motivations for applying to the role. They're also useful in sifting out candidates who are serious about the application and position on offer versus candidates who aren't. Examples of motivational questions include:

- Can you describe a time when you faced a significant challenge? How did you overcome it, and what did you learn?
- What drives you to pursue a career in finance and banking?
- Describe a project or achievement you are particularly proud of. What motivated you to achieve this, and what was the outcome?

PSYCHOMETRIC TESTS

There are many types of psychometric tests that employers all over the world use to test candidates. The most common psychometric tests that financial institutions use are *numerical reasoning tests* (which test your ability to handle and interpret numerical data), *verbal reasoning tests* (which test your ability to understand and comprehend written passages), and *logical reasoning tests* (which test your ability to problem solve and reach a conclusion using logic).

Situational judgement tests (SJTs) are another category of psychometric tests but not as common in the selection process. However, it's good to be aware of them in any case. SJTs aim to measure how well you would perform in a range of different scenarios across a range of social situations and working environments.

INTERVIEWS

There are lots of different types of interviews throughout the selection process. These include:

- online interviews *without* an employee on the other side of the screen
- online interviews *with* an employee on the other side of the screen
- telephone interviews
- individual in-person interviews
- group in-person interviews
- final-round interviews

Although the type of interview is important, it's more important to have a strong understanding of what to prepare for and expect each interview to entail.

There are three main types of interview questions you can expect to be asked when going through the selection process

1. *Competency or behavioural interview questions.* These focus on understanding your ability to learn new skills and how you act and problem solve in certain situations based on your previous academic and/or work experiences. An example of a competency interview question would be: Can you give me an example of a time when you solved a problem in a creative way?

2. *Technical interview questions.* These focus on identifying how much technical knowledge you have that is related to the division or industry that you're applying to. An example of a technical interview question would be: What is discounted cash flow in simple terms?

3. *Brain teasers.* These are less common but worth knowing about. They focus on your ability to quickly arrive at logical conclusions through deductive reasoning. In simple terms, the interviewer will give you a brain teaser and ask you to think out loud whilst solving it. In essence, they want to see how sharp your intuitive thinking skills are.

Online (HireVue) Interviews

Online interviews, known as HireVue interviews (since most firms use the HireVue brand for these interviews), are virtual and don't have an employee or interviewer on the other side of the screen. HireVue interviews test you on your ability to answer a range of competency/behavioural interview questions. The typical format of a HireVue interview includes questions appearing on your screen, followed by a minute to prepare yourself, followed by a minute or two to deliver your answer to the question. Your responses for each question are recorded and the interview is later assessed and reviewed by an employee of the firm.

Telephone Interviews

Telephone interviews used to be more common before the world got used to video calls after the global COVID-19 pandemic in 2020. Personally, I preferred telephone interviews because I didn't have to worry about how I looked, making eye contact, and just generally dealing with interacting face-to-face with another human being. Either way, telephone interviews are still used by many firms in their selection process and typically last around 30 minutes. In terms of the questions that are asked in telephone interviews, for the most part they're behavioural/competency-based interviews. However, you shouldn't be surprised if you're asked a technical question or two.

In-Person Interviews

In-person interviews are, as the name suggests, interviews where you'll be expected to go into the company's offices and participate in a formal interview. However, they can vary by the number of people involved. For example, most in-person interviews consist of two people: you (the interviewee) and an employee (the interviewer—usually someone from human resources or someone from the team that's hiring). Having said this, it isn't uncommon to be interviewed by two people or even three people. In fact, although rare, sometimes interviews can be carried out by a group of employees. Being interviewed by a group of employees would be more common if you were requested to prepare and deliver a presentation or pitch, for example.

Final-Round Interviews

You might be surprised to learn that final-round interviews are actually pretty relaxed. However, that doesn't mean that the stakes are low. The stakes, in fact, are very high. Final-round interviews are the final hurdle before successfully securing an offer. They involve a 30- to 60-minute informal conversation with someone senior within the organisation. This person is most likely to be the managing director or leader of the team that's hiring for the position you've applied for.

The final-round interview isn't like the other interviews you would have participated in as the interviewer isn't going to be asking you tons of behavioural, competency, and technical questions. They trust the judgement of everyone who's already interviewed you and they know by now that you're bright and capable enough to do the work. However, what the final-round interviewer aims to do is to get to know you as a person so they can assess and decide whether they think you'd be a good fit to join their team.

ASSESSMENT CENTRES

You can think of assessment centres as half-day (sometimes full-day) evaluations for you and a group of four to eight other candidates, designed to test how you all interact with each other, solve business-related problems, collaborate and work together, and whether you're a strong fit for the culture of the firm. Assessment centres take place at the offices of the firm and typically consist of the following:

- an opportunity to network with employees and other candidates
- group exercises and case studies
- refreshments and lunch
- individual and group presentations
- role-play exercises
- interviews

They're basically a way for the firm to assess how you would operate in a real-world working environment with other people.

OFFERS AND ACCEPTANCES

Once you've successfully passed every part of the company's selection process you'll be notified by email or phone that the company is excited to give you an offer. They'll either email the contract to you or send it through the post. This contract will lay out all the finer details of your employment with the company. It'll include things like minimum working hours, the location of the office you'll be situated in, pay and benefits, and more. You'll also have a window of time to decide if you want to accept the offer or not.

BACKGROUND CHECKS

Once you sign and send off your contract, the firm will kick off a process behind the scenes. One part of this process includes hiring external companies or vendors who specialise in doing background checks on new employees. These companies will essentially be checking that everything you have said in your application—from your work experience to your academic credentials—is accurate and correct. As well as making sure you haven't lied in your application submission, they're also responsible for making sure the firm isn't at risk of hiring a criminal, for example. So they'll be carrying out criminal record checks as well.

CHAPTER 11

SPRING WEEKS

S pring weeks, sometimes referred to as 'spring insight programmes' or 'insight weeks', have become a crucial stepping stone for students aiming to break into the world of finance and banking careers. These programmes usually take place over a week or two during the Easter break (late March/early to mid-April) and are offered by some of the most prestigious financial institutions in the world, including Goldman Sachs, J.P. Morgan, Morgan Stanley, and Barclays, among others. They're specifically designed for first-year university students (or second-year students on a four-year course) who are eager to get a head start in the industry. Their primary focus is to identify potential talent for the firm's recruitment pipeline, whilst also offering participants an early introduction into the world of work within the financial services sector.

More importantly for you, spring weeks are the easiest route worth taking to secure a summer internship the following year, which, in turn, is the easiest route worth taking to secure a full-time job offer after you graduate. While spring weeks are only a week or two (they vary from firm to firm), they can have a lasting impact on your career trajectory, provide valuable insights into the inner workings of global financial institutions, raise awareness of the range of career opportunities that actually exist for you out there, offer networking opportunities beyond your peers and university cohort, and often lead to summer internships and full-time job offers down the line.

Read on to find out why spring weeks are important, what to expect during a spring week, how to secure one, and more.

WHY SPRING WEEKS ARE IMPORTANT

Spring weeks are more than just a learning opportunity. They're a key part of the graduate recruitment process for the firms that offer them. But let's touch on why they're extremely important for you.

First, they provide early exposure to the industry. With any spring week, you essentially get the keys to the castle. Your key card gives you access to an extremely prestigious organisation that hundreds of thousands of others are competing to break into. A place where some of the sharpest and most technical minds across the financial world work. Spring weeks give you access to all of this, and more. They allow you to understand the different divisions within the firm, the different roles within the divisions, the work culture of the firm, and expectations within the industry. This exposure is invaluable, particularly at such an early stage in your career, in helping you decide whether a career in finance (or within a specific division) is right for you.

Second, they offer solid networking opportunities. During your spring week you'll have the opportunity not only to network with bright students from universities all across the globe but also opportunity to network with industry professionals across seniority levels, from summer interns to recent graduates to senior executives. Building these relationships early on can be incredibly beneficial, as many of these individuals could become mentors, open up new opportunities for you in the future, offer advice, or even help you convert your spring week into a summer internship.

Third, the easiest route to securing a summer internship is by securing a spring week. This is probably the most significant benefit of participating in a spring week. Why? Because a summer internship can eventually lead to a full-time job offer and securing a full-time job without an internship under your belt is extremely difficult, though not impossible. Most banks use spring weeks as an extended interview process, assessing participants' potential for future roles. Typically, at the end of the spring week you'll have an interview which heavily determines whether you'll be receiving an invitation for the firm's summer internship. As such, outperforming during your spring week and acing your end-of-spring-week interview can fast-track you through the recruitment process for summer internships.

Fourth, spring weeks provide the necessary skill development. Spring weeks are designed to help you develop essential skills that are highly valued in finance and banking careers, such as analytical thinking, teamwork, interpersonal skills, leadership, and problem-solving. The hands-on experience and feedback from professionals will give you a head start in building these competencies and give you a sense of what's required in order to succeed at this stage, and later on in your career.

Lastly, doing a spring week significantly boosts your CV. Most students who apply for internships or future finance opportunities aren't as fortunate as those with a spring week listed on their CVs. Why? Because spring weeks indicate drive, initiative, interest, enthusiasm, and a certain level of industry knowledge to recruiters and employees who review summer internship and graduate scheme applications. Doing a spring week signals to future employers that you're serious about a career in finance and have already gained valuable insights and experience in the field. To add to that, let's say you've completed a spring week in asset management. This division-specific spring week will make it easier to secure asset management internship and graduate scheme interviews compared to someone who hasn't completed an asset management spring week.

WHAT TO EXPECT DURING YOUR SPRING WEEK

Although spring weeks can differ from firm to firm, there are common elements that you can expect across most programmes. These include presentations and workshops, shadowing and rotations, case studies and projects, socials and networking events, and an assessment, interview, or presentation with feedback. Let's go through each of these individually.

During your spring week you'll often find yourself sitting in large auditoriums watching presentations from senior executives from across the firm sharing insights about the firm or division, and information aimed to inspire and motivate you for the week or two ahead. Additionally, you'll attend workshops that cover various aspects of the industry, but more specifically focus on the nuances, skills, and knowledge required to succeed in the division that your spring week is focused on. For example, you might attend a valuation and modelling workshop if your spring week is in the investment banking division, whereas you might attend a global markets and trends workshop if your spring week is in the sales and trading division. These workshops are often led by a mix of both junior and senior professionals who share their experiences, insights, and answer any questions you might have for them.

As well as presentations and workshops, spring weeks give you the opportunity to shadow employees carrying out their day-to-day responsibilities. You'll also be given the opportunity to rotate from desk to desk to gain a better understanding of the nature of the work that the employees within the division actually do. Some spring weeks include opportunities to shadow professionals in different divisions. However, most spring weeks centre around the specific division you're doing your spring week in. Either way, this hands-on experience allows you to gain a better understanding of the inner workings of these complex financial institutions.

Next, we have case studies and projects. During the week or two you spend with the firm, you might be given a small case study, individual project, or group project to work on. This task usually requires a combination of networking with employees and leveraging the firm's resources to reach a successful solution to the problem at hand or complete the task at hand. Rest assured, it's not likely to be a substantial piece of work given the limited time you'll have to actually spend working on it. However, it's important you complete it to the best of your ability. Before the end of your spring week, you'll most likely need to present your findings to your peers, HR, and colleagues from the team you worked most closely with.

Spring weeks also offer the opportunity to attend social and networking events. These could be anything from fun socials outside of the office—such as table tennis or bowling—to internal networking 'lunch and learn' sessions. Socials and networking events are great as they allow you to connect with colleagues from all seniority levels, ask questions, and learn from others' experiences in a less formal setting.

Last but not least, as briefly mentioned above, you'll experience an assessment, interview, or presentation with feedback towards the end of your spring week. These are all used to assess and evaluate your suitability for the firm and for future roles within the division or team you spent time with during your spring week. If successful, you'll be offered a place on the organisation's summer internship programme for the following year.

HOW TO SECURE A SPRING WEEK

Given the extremely competitive nature of spring weeks, it's essential to approach the application process strategically and as early as possible. Let's go through some tips to help you stand out and secure a place on a spring week programme.

You want to be ready and able to put together a strong application as soon as firms start accepting applications. The reason for this is twofold. Firstly, offers are handed out on a rolling basis and once they're gone, they're gone. Thus, the earlier you apply, the better your chances of securing an offer. Secondly, given the competitive nature of spring weeks, places do tend to fill up pretty quickly. As such, leaving it too late to apply simply means there's a higher chance of not being successful as places might have already been offered to other candidates. Therefore, keep an eye on application deadlines and start preparations (writing your CV, writing your cover letter, practising online psychometric tests, etc.) as early as possible.

In order to stand out among the sea of candidates who apply to spring weeks, you need to be able to customise and tailor your application to each firm you apply to. Yes, this can seem quite arduous and long-winded; however, the alternative is to take the easy approach and write generic applications which are highly likely to get rejected. The choice is yours. So, what does tailoring your application actually mean? Well, what you want to do is research the firm's website, social media presence, recent news and developments, culture and values, areas of expertise and strength, and so on, and reflect your understanding of some of these things in your CV and cover letter. To add to that, you want to highlight any relevant course work, skills, work experience, extracurricular activities, or voluntary experiences that demonstrate your interest in the world of finance.

Strong academic performance is a key factor that many firms and employees will consider when reviewing applications. Though they aren't the be all and end all, they play an important role in helping your application get noticed and put through to the next stage of the hiring process. So it's important to keep in mind, while grades aren't the only consideration, they can be the difference between you and another candidate that the firm is stuck deciding between. Therefore, you should focus on acing your pre-university and university exams, maintaining a high average grade throughout academia, and focus on relevant subjects such as economics, finance, and maths, if they're of particular interest.

I always encourage students and graduates to remember that your academic experience will only take up a few lines at the top of your CV. The rest of your CV will focus on what you did outside of your academic studies. As such, it's imperative to secure as much relevant experience as you can if you want a chance at securing the most competitive roles. Ideally, you want to secure some relevant finance and banking experience before applying, even if it's through extracurricular activities, part-time work, or volunteering. Doing so means you'll be able to talk about it on your CV and highlight the skills you've learned, the results you've achieved, and flag to the reader that you've taken the initiative to gain such experience because you're genuinely interested in a career within the world of finance and banking. When you're in university you can further build on your experience by joining finance societies, investment clubs, and so on that further demonstrate your commitment to the field. And always remember, anyone can simply be a member of a society or club, but you'll learn a lot more (and it's more impressive) if you take on an active leadership position instead.

If you submit an application and pass the initial CV and cover letter review, you'll likely be invited to complete a number of online psychometric tests. The most common three are the numerical reasoning, verbal reasoning, and logical reasoning tests. These are timed (they usually give you 20 minutes to complete

20 multiple choice questions) tests that test your ability to think quickly under pressure. The only way to pass these tests is through lots of practice, never second-guessing yourself or changing an answer, pacing yourself, and not spending too much time on any given question. The good thing is you can search and access lots of free and paid practise psychometric tests online, which I would highly recommend you do sooner rather than later.

When you get to the interview stage, be ready to discuss your interest in finance, your understanding of the industry, and why you're interested in that particular division. On top of this, be prepared to answer a battery of competency-based questions that focus on the skills learned and developed on the back of your previous experiences and how they've equipped you with the skills required to succeed in a career in the world of finance.

Lastly, you can never network enough. Whether it be during in-person events at company offices or online through email and/or LinkedIn, networking is always useful. Therefore, you should make an active effort to build connections and relationships with successful peers and individuals already in the industry. Keep in mind, it's always easier to network with people who have a mutual affiliation with you. This mutual affiliation might be someone you both know, but it doesn't necessarily have to be a person. Your shared mutual affiliation could be the fact that you went to the same school, or that they're an alumni of your university, or that you both studied the same subject, or anything else that makes it easier to reach out to them and break the ice. You can find out most of this information by searching on LinkedIn.

Alternatively, if you're at an in-person networking event, be sure to make an effort to actively engage and talk to people. You'll be surprised at how much information you can come away with after a short conversation with someone whom you connect well with. Once you're comfortable networking and have successfully nurtured a few relationships with industry professionals or successful spring interns (or even summer interns), ask if they would kindly review your CV and cover letter for you. If you've built a strong relationship with an industry professional, don't be afraid to ask them if they're okay with you mentioning them in your cover letter. After all, name-dropping in your cover letter is a simple way to stand out as it shows you've taken the initiative to actually connect with someone from the firm you're applying to. If you're wondering how to 'name-drop' someone, you simply mention them in your cover letter in a sentence explaining something positive that they've told or taught you about the company or division.

MAKING THE MOST OF YOUR SPRING WEEK

Once you've secured a place on a spring week, it's important to put your best foot forward and make the most of the experience. Here are five tips I would encourage you to focus on throughout the duration of your spring week in order to get the most out of it:

- be proactive
- network actively
- seek feedback
- reflect on your experience
- stay connected

Let's go through them one by one.

Be proactive. You want to show people that you're a go-getter and can take initiative during your time at the firm. A simple way to do this is to regularly ask questions, seek out additional learning opportunities, and show enthusiasm by offering your time even when it's not been requested (i.e. frequently, but not annoyingly, asking team members if there's anything you can help them with or take off their plate). The more proactive and engaged you are, the more you'll get out of the experience.

Network actively. Try to network with as many people as possible. Understanding that you'll only be at the firm for a very limited time will help you see the bigger picture and appreciate the value of networking and building connections. As such, you should attend all networking events, introduce yourself to professionals, and follow up with an email (thanking them for their time or asking for 30 minutes of their time for a catch-up) later on to nurture the relationship. Doing these seemingly small and effortless tasks early on, and doing them consistently over a long period of time, really does pay dividends as many of your professional relationships will likely open doors to future opportunities for you that you might otherwise have never come across.

Seek feedback. Many students don't do this enough. Don't be afraid to ask for feedback on your performance on a particular exercise or task. Understanding your strengths and areas for improvement will only help you grow. Furthermore, displaying a growth mindset is what these firms want in their employees. If you're able to show them you're willing to accept constructive criticism and act upon it to improve, they're more likely to offer you a place on the summer programme.

Reflect on your experience. After you've completed your spring week, it's important to take some time to reflect. Ask yourself what you have learned and how it all aligns with your longer-term career goals. Did you like the nature of the work they had you doing? Can you see yourself doing this type of work for the next 1, 5, 10, or even 40 years after you graduate? By asking yourself these questions and taking time to reflect on your experience you'll be better positioned to make more informed future decisions, whether it's applying for summer internships in a different division or deciding you'd much rather explore career opportunities in a different industry altogether.

Stay connected. It's always a good idea to stay connected with the people you meet on your spring week. That means keeping in touch with the other participants on the spring week, the employees you meet across the firm, the employees you worked most closely with, the HR professionals who organised and assisted you throughout the spring week, and anyone else you feel you might have connected well with. And always remember, a simple follow-up email thanking someone for their time and insights or advice can go a long way in maintaining these relationships.

Spring weeks are a golden opportunity for you to gain early exposure and access to the world of finance and banking, build valuable networks, and set the foundation for a successful career in this industry. While the application process is rigorous and competitive, to say the least, with careful preparation and a proactive approach, you'll be able to secure a spot in one of these prestigious programmes. Remember, the effort you put into your spring week can pay off significantly, potentially leading to a summer internship, and then a full-time role, and essentially a clear path to a thriving career in finance.

CHAPTER 12

INTERNSHIPS

SUMMER INTERNSHIPS AND OFF-CYCLE INTERNSHIPS

Internships are an essential part of launching a career in finance, providing crucial experience, networking opportunities, and a pathway to full-time roles. However, not all internships are the same, and understanding the differences between summer internships and off-cycle internships can help you choose the best path for landing a full-time offer and building a career in the world of finance. With this in mind, let's go through some of the key differences between summer internships and off-cycle internships.

Duration and Timing

Summer internships typically occur during the summer (June, July, August) and last 8–10 weeks depending on the firm. These internships are designed to coincide with the academic calendar, making them ideal for students who want to gain experience without interfering with their studies.

Off-cycle internships, on the other hand, can take place at any time of the year and vary in duration, ranging from a few weeks to several months. They tend to be more flexible and can accommodate students who are taking a gap year or graduates who are looking to gain experience outside of the traditional recruiting season.

Recruitment Process

The recruitment process for summer internships is highly structured and competitive, often starting up to a year in advance. Some firms open their applications as early as May the year before the summer internship is to take place, and the expectation is for candidates to submit a CV, cover letter, pass a battery of online psychometric tests, participate in multiple rounds of interviews, and attend an assessment centre, before receiving an offer. The hiring process for off-cycle internships is typically more ad hoc, with openings filled as and when firms need extra support. This means that off-cycle roles might be advertised with little notice, and the recruitment process is usually quicker, often involving fewer stages.

Objectives and Opportunities

Summer internships serve as a key pipeline for full-time analyst positions at most investment banks. These firms use internships to evaluate potential hires, often extending full-time job offers to top performers before they return to university for their final year. In contrast, off-cycle internships are usually not as directly tied to full-time recruitment pipelines. They're often used to fill immediate needs within a team, such as during a busy period or when there's a short-term project that requires additional resources. While off-cycle internships can lead to full-time offers, the pathway is less structured, and these roles are more about gaining experience and proving your worth on an as-needed basis.

Work Experience and Exposure

Both types of internships offer valuable experience, but the nature of the work can differ. As a summer intern you'll often follow a structured programme with a blend of training sessions, networking events, and projects designed to give you a comprehensive overview of the firm and its operations. As an off-cycle intern you might not receive the same formal training but can gain more hands-on experience and potentially take on more responsibility, as you'll often work directly on live projects with less oversight and structure. This can be a great way to build your practical skills quickly, though it can also mean a steeper learning curve.

Networking and Culture

Networking opportunities can also differ between the two types of internships. Summer internships generally include numerous networking events, social activities, and mentorship programmes, allowing interns to build relationships across the divisions and teams within divisions. Off-cycle interns might miss out on some of these formal networking opportunities, but they have the advantage of working closely with their teams and building deeper relationships through day-to-day collaboration. This can lead to strong personal connections and mentoring opportunities, especially in smaller teams or less formal settings. Each intern will have the ability to proactively network and organise catch-ups on their own with people across the firm; however, the summer internship programmes are structured to offer more of these opportunities without proactively seeking them out yourself.

Summary

Both summer internships and off-cycle internships offer valuable pathways into careers across the world of finance and banking, each with its own set of advantages and disadvantages. Summer internships provide a more structured experience and a clear path to full-time employment, making them ideal for students on a traditional academic schedule. For those of you who aren't on a traditional academic schedule, off-cycle internships might be more suitable. While less formalised, they offer flexibility and the chance to gain varied experience and responsibility throughout the year. Depending on your personal situation and career goals, either of these is an excellent way to get your foot in the door.

THE IMPORTANCE OF SUMMER INTERNSHIPS

If you're looking to break into the world of finance, securing a summer internship is one of the most important steps you can take. A summer internship is essentially an extended interview, a test run for both you and the firm to see if there's a fit. Unlike spring weeks, which are shorter and more exploratory, summer internships are typically 8–10 weeks long and offer a deep dive into a particular division (which you would have specifically applied to), providing hands-on experience and exposure to the fast-paced environment within a global investment bank. If you're serious about a career in the world of banking and finance, a summer internship is your golden ticket to a full-time role after you graduate. It's not just about learning the ropes. It's about proving yourself in a real-world setting, showing that you're a strong fit for the culture of the firm and the team, and being able to successfully work with others to reach a common goal.

Summer internships are structured programmes offered by a range of financial institutions including investment banks, asset managers, hedge funds, and more. These programmes are primarily targeted at penultimate-year university students who are about to enter their final year of study (i.e. second-year students completing a three-year degree, third-year students completing a four-year degree, or final-year students who will be doing a Master's degree after they graduate).

The goal of an internship is to give you a taste of what it's like to work in the world of finance and, more importantly, to assess your potential for a full-time role after graduation. During a summer internship, you'll join a specific team or division. However, if you're on the trading floor it's not uncommon for you to frequently rotate and move from desk to desk rather than stick with one team for the full 8- to 10-week internship experience. You'll also be given the opportunity to work on live projects, attend meetings, and contribute to the team's overall goals. One of the great things about interning at an investment bank, and something I particularly enjoyed during my time interning within the asset management division of Goldman Sachs, is that they get you involved in 'real' work. For example, the work you produce will play a part in helping the team produce work, save time, or save money for a client. This can, and should, be empowering for any intern. After all, most of us would rather be useful than do pointless work just for the sake of being present.

Having said this, the internship is an extremely intense period since you'll be working on a ton of different projects and requests all at the same time, whilst also trying to network with colleagues, explore other teams and divisions, manage regular catch-ups, seek feedback, focus on completing your own internship projects and assignments to the best of your ability, learn as much about the division and your line of work as possible, and more. As such, the learning curve is often quite steep, and the experience you gain as a result of being 'thrown in at the deep end' can be invaluable. You'll be stressed at times, but this is the training ground that prepares you for the world of work better than any other industry. By the end of the programme, your manager and team will have a good sense of your capabilities, and you'll have a much clearer idea of whether this career path is right for you.

Why Summer Internships Are Important

Summer internships are more than just a CV booster. They're a critical step in launching your career in finance. Here's why securing a summer internship is so vital and important in achieving your early career goals.

First, they provide a direct pathway into full-time roles. For most firms, summer internships are the main pipeline for full-time graduate positions. A strong performance during your internship will lead to a full-time job offer, so you won't need to worry about applying for graduate schemes or taking part in any future graduate recruitment hiring processes. To add to that, most investment banks hire the majority of their full-time analysts from their pool of summer interns. As a result, it becomes even more difficult—given the heightened level of competition—to land a full-time graduate offer without completing an internship beforehand.

Second, internships give you hands-on, real-life experience. Unlike spring weeks, where you'll partake in menial tasks and projects, and which tend to be more observational, summer internships offer the chance to do real work. You're not just shadowing someone. Instead, you're actively contributing to projects, attending client meetings, and working alongside experienced professionals. This hands-on experience, and the skills you'll learn as a result of it, is crucial for building the practical skills you'll need in a full-time role.

Third, you will have an extended period to explore networking opportunities. The longer duration of a summer internship allows you to build deeper relationships within the firm (and across multiple teams and divisions). You'll have the chance to network not only with your peers and junior professionals but also with senior executives. These connections can lead to mentoring opportunities, invaluable career advice, and open doors to future opportunities within the firm and broader financial services industry.

Fourth, you'll be developing relevant skills. Over the course of your internship, you'll develop a range of skills that are essential in finance careers. These include analytical thinking, financial modelling (if working in the investment banking division), teamwork, communication, and problem-solving, to name a few. The intensive nature of a summer internship forces you to learn quickly and apply what you've learned in a high-pressure environment. The more of this you do, the better you'll get at the given skills being used. This will set you apart from the competition and any candidates who haven't completed an internship and will be useful should you decide to apply for full-time roles outside of the firm you interned with.

Fifth, doing an internship offers a unique insight and exposure to the firm's culture. This is important because cultural fit plays a big part in whether you enjoy and succeed in any given role over the long term. During your internship, you'll get a sense of the firm's work culture, the type of people that work at the company, their values, and their expectations. This information will be extremely useful in helping you decide whether this firm, or division, is the right place for you to start building your career. A point worth mentioning is that it's not uncommon for different divisions within the same investment bank to have different cultures. For example, the trading floor is more likely to be an intense and highly pressurised environment, with individuals who communicate directly and can often come across as rude or blunt. In contrast, you might experience less of this direct and blunt communication style in the asset management division, where the nature of the work isn't as fast paced and intense as it is on the trading floor.

Finally, an internship offers an opportunity to be exposed to regular feedback, which can contribute to professional growth. Throughout your internship, you'll receive feedback from your managers and peers on the work you've completed or been a part of. This feedback is crucial for your professional development as it gives you direction and guidance on how you can get to the 'next level'. Additionally, understanding what you're doing well and where you need to improve as an intern will help you grow and better prepare you for a full-time role.

What to Expect

Summer internships are intensive, and each firm structures its programme differently. However, there are some common elements you can expect across most internships. These include:

- orientation and training
- assigned projects and tasks
- team collaboration
- networking events
- performance reviews
- social events and team-building activities
- final presentation or project

Let's go through them one by one.

Orientation and training. Most internships start with orientation and training, otherwise known as induction week. This can range from a few days to a full week and is designed to get you up to speed with the firm's systems, tools, and processes. As well as this, you'll learn about the firm's history, its culture, and the specific division you'll be working in by attending multiple presentations and networking events alongside your intern class. You might also receive technical training on topics like financial modelling and valuation, financial accounting, Microsoft Excel, and financial markets analysis, but this will depend on the division you're interning in.

Assigned projects and tasks. After you meet the team and your colleagues, you'll be given real work from the get-go. You'll be given real projects and tasks to work on and these could range from conducting market research, preparing materials for internal or external meetings, doing financial analysis to preparing pitch books, and more. The specific work you do will depend on the division you're interning in as well as the varying needs of the team. Expect to be challenged, as firms want to see how well you can handle pressure and whether you can deliver to a high standard under such pressure. Oftentimes, the internship is actually more intense (purely because you have so much going on) than the actual job after you graduate.

Team collaboration. Throughout your internship you'll be working closely with a team of analysts, associates, and sometimes even more senior professionals like vice presidents, directors, and managing directors. Teamwork is highly valued across this industry, and your ability to work well with others will be closely observed. As such, make sure you're keeping people updated on the things you're working on, ask for deadlines so you don't prolong the work required on a particular task, and always under-promise but over-deliver (i.e. let them know you'll get the work to them by a certain time and date, but be sure to surprise them by completing the work to a high standard well ahead of time). The simplest way to win people over in this industry is to save them time and produce high-quality work. If you do this, and do it often, it'll be hard for the team to not give you a full-time offer.

Networking events. As well as an expectation to collaborate effectively with your team, during your internship you'll be expected to attend a number of networking events. During these events or sessions, you'll have multiple opportunities to network with people from across the firm, and across seniority levels. These events could take the form of formal networking events, speaker series, or informal coffee chats. Either way, you want to make the most of these opportunities so you can learn from others and begin nurturing important relationships. Sometimes, an intern ends up not enjoying the nature of the work in the team they're interning in, but because they've successfully networked with someone senior from a different division (or team within the same division) they've been able to explore opportunities and successfully secure an offer within a different team. Networking isn't just about getting a job or using people for your own benefit. It's about learning from the experiences of those around you, offering your time and knowledge or insights, and building a support system within the industry. The earlier you start building your network and industry support system, the sooner you'll be able to reap the rewards of being so well connected.

Performance reviews. A pivotal part of the internship is the intern performance review. It's an opportunity to learn about and receive constructive feedback on your strengths and weaknesses, or areas for development. You'll be asked by your manager to send a list of people you've been working closely with over the first few weeks of your internship so your manager can reach out to them for feedback on working with you. After everyone submits feedback to your manager, you'll have a meeting (usually with your manager and a buddy or mentor in the room as well) to discuss the feedback.

What's most important about the internship performance review is what you do after it's done. For example, you could have had the worst start to your internship, and it could be reflected in your performance review, with tons of negative feedback and constructive criticism. However, you'll still be able to go ahead and secure a full-time offer if you're able to do one particular thing between your feedback review and the end of your internship. All you have to do is show your manager, the team, and the people who submitted feedback on you that you can take constructive criticism, act upon it, make the necessary changes, and improve. Displaying the ability to grow and develop is what firms and divisions want in candidates.

The last thing they want is a candidate who throws a strop or whines because all of the feedback wasn't positive. Whatever you do, don't be that intern. Listen to the feedback and get to work on improving in the respective areas as soon as possible. Take the performance review seriously, prepare to discuss what you've learned over the previous few weeks, what you're proud of, and areas where you'd like to improve. Doing so will show your manager that you're mature enough and suitable for a full-time role.

Social events and team-building activities. Internships aren't just about work. Firms often organise social events and team-building activities to help interns bond and to give you a feel of the company culture. It's also a nice opportunity to relax and enjoy an evening out with everyone, especially after the weeks of hard work and effort all the interns have been put through. These events can range from bowling to ping-pong and are a great way to get to know your peers and colleagues in a more relaxed setting. There's always an intern or two who overindulges in the unlimited alcohol on offer at social events. My advice here would be to avoid being that intern as it can really destroy your chances of converting your internship into a full-time offer and will ruin your reputation (word travels fast not just within each division or firm, but across the industry). Although social events and team-building activities can seem informal, always remember that you're still being assessed and are essentially part of an 8- to 10-week interview process.

Final presentation or project. This is something which you would have spent the majority of your internship working on. This is your chance to showcase what you've learned and the work you've done during your time at the firm. You'll be expected to present in front of everyone you've worked with or built a relationship with throughout your internship, which can seem quite daunting. The good news is that public speaking is just a confidence issue. And the way to increase your confidence when it comes to presentations and public speaking is to become an expert on the topic and know what you're talking about. In regard to your presentation, this means spending a solid amount of time working on your project and also practising presenting it.

Here are three important tips when it comes to your final presentation. First, you want to book the date in your calendar (and start inviting people to your presentation) as early as possible (try to have this done by week two of your internship). The reason for doing this is that all the other interns will also have final presentations which they'll want a lot of the same people to attend (you'll all meet lots of people across the division). By setting a date early, you'll have the first pick in everyone's calendars. Second, aim to do your final presentation on the penultimate week of your internship. By doing so, you'll have one final week to spend time networking and doing final catch-ups, doing desk work and anything else that isn't final project related. This is the best way to use your time at the end of your internship, as opposed to slugging away working on your presentation. Third, plant a question or two in your final presentation: ask one or two people you can trust (it can be your buddy, mentor, or a fellow intern) to ask you a question during your final presentation that you already know the answer to. Everyone does this, and it's a simple and straightforward way of building your confidence whilst aiding your performance.

How to Secure a Summer Internship

Given the competitive nature of summer internships, it's essential to approach the application process strategically. I often share the following advice with students for standing out and securing a spot in one's preferred division:

- start early
- tailor your application
- practise online tests
- prepare for interviews
- leverage your network
- identify your value proposition
- demonstrate your passion

Let's go into more detail on each one.

Start early. Applications for summer internships often open as early as the summer before the academic year, and positions can fill up quickly given that they're offered on a rolling basis. What this means is that rather than waiting for the deadline and then reading every application before handing out offers, firms will hand out offers as soon as possible (even before reaching the application deadline) to candidates they deem suitable for the role. Therefore, I highly recommend starting your application preparation a few months before applications open. By preparing this early, you'll be miles ahead of most applicants who apply two or three months after the opening date and as a result you'll be more likely to secure offers across the board. Also, keep an eye out for application trackers (visit www.afzalhussein.com to explore them) so you're aware of when deadlines and key dates for internships are.

Tailor your application. When preparing for applications, you want to dedicate a large amount of time crafting a strong CV and cover letter. More importantly, you need to get good at tailoring your application by customising your CV and cover letter for each firm you apply to. The most important rule to remember is, the more specific your application is to each firm you apply to, the higher your chances of successfully securing an interview. You want to highlight any relevant experiences, skills, and achievements that demonstrate your interest in finance (or the division) and why they make you suitable for the role. To add to that, you want to show that you've done your homework by mentioning specifics about the firm. This could range from the firm's culture to their values or recent achievements and milestones you've discovered in the press or on their website. Most candidates don't do this level of research, but even those who do attempt to make their cover letters or CVs specific in this way only carry out the most basic level of research, which comes across as lazy. The aim of doing specific research on any firm is to impress the reader with the depth of research that you've gone and carried out. This is what separates the standout candidates from the sea of average candidates.

Practise online tests. Making sure you get in enough practice for online psychometric tests is vital for you to successfully secure a summer internship. These tests are often the bane of many students' existence, but they're something you simply can't avoid. If you want to progress in the application after submitting your CV and cover letter, most firms will require you to complete a range of tests including, but not limited to, verbal reasoning, numerical reasoning, situational judgement, and logical reasoning. These are all timed multiple-choice tests, usually spanning 20 minutes each, and you'll have around 20 questions to answer. Pass marks are often in the high teens (think at least 17 out of 20) and the only way to ace these tests is through thorough online practice beforehand. I've learned over time that the more tests you do, the less daunting they'll become as you become more familiar with their structure and layout, the faster you'll get at answering the questions, and the accuracy of your calculations will improve too. It's just a numbers game: do more tests, learn from your mistakes, and improve over time.

Prepare for interviews. If you make it to the interview stage, be ready to discuss your interest in finance, your understanding of the industry, and why you're interested in the specific firm and division. What's more, it's always important to have your own story nailed down. What do I mean by this? Well, not many students give this enough thought, but it's basically all about having a short outline (story) of what's brought you into the interview room at that exact point in time. The story that I told interviewers when prompted (*tell me about yourself*) went something like this:

> I grew up in a household of five siblings all raised on benefits (government-funded income support) in a council estate (government-funded housing) by my mother, a single parent. Growing up, I always

knew I wanted to put on a suit and work in the city, but I didn't really know what jobs actually existed within the world of financial services. And growing up in a council estate meant that I didn't have any connections, friends, or cousins working in the industry that I could reach out to. So during my A-levels I decided to try to learn as much as I could about the world of finance careers as possible, and hopefully when in university secure some experience along the way in order to get some real-life, hands-on experience to teach me what I liked or was good at, versus what I didn't like or wasn't so good at. When I got to university, I discovered spring week programmes and my strategy was simple. I wanted to get as much exposure to the different areas across the world of finance as possible. As such, in my first year I completed spring weeks across operations, audit, trading, and asset management. After completing these experiences, I realised I was best suited for, and most enjoyed, working in and learning about the world of asset management. It was a combination of the interpersonal nature of the world of asset management and a focus on long-term client relationships, as well as the level of technical expertise asset management professionals are expected to have that attracted me to focus all of my summer internship applications on asset management. And that's kind of how I ended up in this seat today.

Your story has two main objectives. First, it should give the interviewer some context. Context tells them who you are, where you come from, and how you've become interested in the world of finance. Essentially, context paints a picture and makes everything a little clearer. Second, it should give the interviewer a sense of your strengths and illustrate your natural ability to take initiative and go after the things that you're most interested in. A story that does these two things sets you up for a strong interview.

Leverage your network. Reach out to professionals already working in the industry, alumni, or contacts from previous spring weeks for insights and advice. If you've completed a spring week before, you should have an extensive network to rely on. If you haven't completed a spring week,

I would suggest first reaching out to industry professionals (you're most likely to hear back from analysts and associates) who have attended your university or studied the same degree as you. It always helps to find some sort of mutual connection (degree subject, school, university, friends, etc.) when trying to reach out and connect to someone for the first time.

Identify your value proposition. You don't always need one but believe me it really does help to have a unique strength or unfair advantage that sets you apart from the rest of the crowd applying for the same role. In most cases, value propositions are quite technical. For example, you might be able to say you're a strong financial modeller, trader, or portfolio manager, and then back this up with strong examples and results achieved (i.e. winning competitions or having completed extensive work experience). These are highly relevant for technical roles such as investment banking, trading, and portfolio management. If you have these strengths, they'll give you an unfair advantage over the competition. If you don't have them, it's not the end of the world, but pitching yourself for such roles might be harder to do. Try and find your unfair advantage or value proposition. What do you bring to the table and how can you provide value to the team? Answer these questions and you'll be one step closer to securing that all-important offer.

Demonstrate your passion. Whether through your academic studies, extracurricular activities, or work experience, you want the person or people opposite you to know that you're genuinely interested in this industry. Join finance clubs (but don't just be a member, take on an active leadership position), participate in relevant competitions, trade financial securities (stocks, bonds, etc.) using a free online demo account, carry out unique research or do a university project on a related field, seek out finance experiences, and keep up-to-date with what's going on in the broader financial markets as well as specifically to the division you're most interested in. Anyone who sees these things on your CV will immediately assume you're serious about breaking into the industry.

Making the Most of It

Once you've secured a summer internship, it's crucial to make the most of the experience. Similar to making the most of your spring week, you want to do the same things to make the most of your summer internship. These include:

- being proactive
- networking actively
- seeking feedback
- reflecting on your performance
- staying organised and managing your time effectively
- showcasing your skills and achievements
- being adaptable and open to learning
- staying connected

Let's go through them one by one.

Being proactive means not waiting to be told what to do. Take the initiative to ask questions, seek out additional learning opportunities, and offer to help with tasks and projects. The more you put in, the more you'll get out of the experience.

Networking actively is all about using your extended time at the firm to build relationships with your peers, your team, and professionals from other divisions (across seniority levels). These connections will prove hugely useful after your internship ends. Attend networking events, reach out for coffee chats or catch-ups, and don't be afraid to introduce yourself to new people. Networking is one of the most valuable aspects of a summer internship and can open doors to future opportunities.

Seeking feedback from your colleagues on work you complete for them is vital. It'll help you understand what you're doing right and what you need to focus a little more time and attention on. Additionally, regularly *reflecting on your performance* will allow you to discover other ways and areas (hard skills and/or soft skills) that you can improve.

Staying organised and managing your time effectively is vital for success. Summer internships can be demanding, with multiple projects, deadlines, and tasks to juggle. Always keep a 'to-do' list close by so you know where you are with the things that need to be done and never take on more than you can manage. The last thing you want as an intern is to be identified as the intern that lets things fall through the gaps/doesn't complete things when they're meant to.

Showcasing your skills and achievements is important. Whether it's through your work on a project, a presentation, or a final report, make sure you're showcasing your abilities and the value you bring to the team. Doing so doesn't need to be done in an arrogant, 'everyone, look at how great I am' kind of way. All you need to do is regularly post your manager (send them updates) on how you're progressing or how your internship experience is going. One simple way of doing this, which I did during my summer internship, is to send a one-page email summary to your manager at the end of each week listing the different things you worked on, tasks you completed, meetings you attended, people you met, and so on.

Being adaptable and open to learning is indispensable in the dynamic world of finance and banking. Things can change quickly. Therefore, it's important to be adaptable, always remain open to learning new things, and be willing to take on new challenges. If you do so, your willingness to learn and adapt will be noticed and appreciated by your team.

Staying connected with the people you meet builds your network and shows initiative. Send a thank-you note to your manager and any colleagues who you felt added to your internship experience. And don't forget to connect with your colleagues on LinkedIn whilst the relationships are still warm. Last but not least, make an active effort to keep in touch with the firm's or division's recruitment team. It's always useful to have connections in the hiring process. Human resource professionals often move firms within the same industry and maintaining such relationships can help you stay top-of-mind for future opportunities.

Summary

A summer internship is a critical step in launching your finance career. It offers invaluable experience, exposure, and networking opportunities that can set you up for success in the industry. Additionally, it offers you an 8- to 10-week stint at a world-class financial institution to explore and decide whether a career in this industry, or the particular division you're interning in, is where you want to be after you graduate. Whether the industry is right for you or not, I always encourage students to take advantage of the experience and make the most of it. After all, you should always try to make the most of opportunities that aren't easily offered to everyone. You never know what you might learn, who you might meet, or how the experience might change the future trajectory of your life.

By preparing thoroughly, engaging fully, and leveraging the opportunities available to you, you can make the most of your summer internship and set yourself on a path to a rewarding career in finance. Remember, your internship isn't just about learning. It's an extended interview offering the opportunity to prove yourself in a work environment, build your network across a global financial institution, and position yourself for future success in an ever-changing industry. Make the most of it, and you'll be well on your way to securing that coveted full-time return offer. For specific resources on how to stand out and convert your summer internship into a full-time role visit www.afzalhussein.com.

CHAPTER 13

GRADUATE SCHEMES

G raduate schemes are highly competitive and securing a position on a graduate scheme becomes significantly more challenging if you haven't participated in a spring week or internship. I frequently come across students in their final year of university, wondering how to secure graduate schemes. Yet, when I review their CVs, I find that they've either forgotten or ignored the importance of completing a spring week or an internship before reaching their final year of academia. Let this be a crucial reminder: if you're in your first or second year, you need to prioritise building your CV with spring weeks and internships in order to make securing a graduate scheme easier. If you find yourself in your final year without having done a spring week or internship, rest assured it's not the end of the world though; you can still break into the industry.

The easiest route into a graduate scheme is as follows: you complete a spring week, convert your spring week into a summer internship, outperform on your summer internship, and then convert your summer internship into a full-time offer onto the firm's graduate scheme. I can't stress enough how important it is to start early. The earlier you begin your career preparation, the less hassle the entire process will be for you.

In contrast, applying directly to graduate schemes without any prior experience, internships, or spring weeks will prove a lot more difficult. Why? Well, think of it like this. You'll be competing with students from elite universities, from all over the world, who already have multiple internship and spring week experiences under their belts. And if this alone doesn't make it extremely competitive, throw in the fact that you'll also be competing with postgraduate students who are completing their Master's degrees in finance and investment-related fields.

That's why my advice to any and every student interested in breaking into the world of finance and banking is to focus on securing a graduate scheme by first completing an internship. The interviews, assessments, expectations, and entry requirements for securing an internship are a lot easier and lower for candidates than they are for direct graduate scheme applications.

For those of you reading this in your final year of university or completing a Master's degree, and your only option is to apply directly to graduate schemes, then the key focus for you would be to build your CV, prioritising the following and in the following order: relevant experience, relevant certifications like the CFA (Chartered Financial Analyst), IMC (Investment Management Certificate), and so on, relevant projects, irrelevant experience highlighting relevant skills, and extracurricular activities.

You should also consider applying to less competitive roles such as those in the middle or back office of investment banks, whilst also looking into other industries such as consulting or professional services. By doing so, you'll still have a chance to break into your desired role after a few years of solid networking and strong performance in whichever role you pursue straight out of university. To add to that, these roles receive fewer applications, tend to be less technical, and are often easier to break into compared to the more popular front-office divisions. This might be a hard pill to swallow, particularly as most students want to work in the front office because of the 'fancier' roles, client-facing aspects, higher compensation and bonuses, and solid exit opportunities. However, it's important to be realistic about your early career prospects based on your current situation and experiences on your CV compared to the competition.

If you do go ahead and prioritise applying to middle and back-office roles and still hope to one day move into the front office, I would encourage you to apply to either the risk or operations divisions. These divisions work closely with the front-office divisions in order to ensure smooth operations and risk management. For example, when trades are executed, the operations teams make sure everything checks out on the back end, or when a client invests capital into a portfolio, the risk management team will monitor various aspects of the portfolio to ensure the client funds are protected, and the list goes on. The point I'm trying to make here is that if you want to move into the front office, it makes sense to have a route or be on a path that will get you there. As such, it makes more sense to break into risk or operations as opposed to technology or human resources in order to eventually make the move into investment banking, sales and trading, asset management, or private wealth management. Therefore, when applying to graduate schemes try to take a three- to five-year strategic view by stepping back and thinking about the big picture. The last thing you want is to be the graduate with no experience who only applied to front-office roles and ended up with nothing.

STRUCTURE OF GRADUATE SCHEMES

The typical structure of a graduate scheme can vary from firm to firm, and from division to division. For example, at some investment banks you'll be part of a rotational programme where the graduate scheme will last for two years, and you'll complete four rotations (working with different teams within the division) spanning six months each. At the end of the four rotations, you'll have a say in which team you enjoyed working with most, and if they share the same sentiment, you'll join that team full time.

The alternative is a less-structured graduate scheme, where you might be placed directly into a role with no formal graduate scheme structure (i.e. no rotations). In such cases, you typically join the team you completed an internship with (this was what happened in my case at Goldman Sachs) or the team you applied for (if you didn't complete an internship at the firm). There's no formal training or structured graduate programme; you're simply expected to hit the ground running and kick-start your career.

CAREER PROGRESSION

When you join a firm on their graduate scheme, you typically start as an analyst. You'll generally be an analyst for two to three years (this can vary from firm to firm and division to division) before you're able to be promoted to the associate level. Having said this, it's important to note that promotions in the world of banking and finance aren't a guaranteed rite of passage as they depend heavily on numerous factors, including, but not limited to, your individual performance, growth and development, commercial awareness, and commercial contributions. Essentially, you need to be a top performer if you want a guaranteed promotion.

WORK–LIFE BALANCE

Lastly, when you start your graduate scheme in the front office, you can expect your working hours during the graduate scheme to be fairly demanding. You're in the real world now, where you're doing real work and working on live deals, transactions, investments in the multi-millions, and essentially serving some of the world's most prominent businesses, institutions, governments, and individuals. The industry you've entered rarely offers a nine to five, but in exchange offers an envious compensation package with many perks. As such, you can expect to work five days a week (some firms prefer you to be in the office every day, others offer some flexibility, but the general trend in the industry post-pandemic is at least three days a week in the office), with hours ranging from 12- to 18-hour days in the front office (18-hour shifts [e.g. 9 am to 3 am] aren't uncommon in the investment banking division in your first two years, whilst you can expect to do a 6 am to 7 pm in sales and trading and a 7:30 am to 8 pm in asset management).

Keep in mind, workloads do vary from time to time as quarter ends, holiday seasons, earnings seasons, and so on can affect you and your team. Think of it like this, when you're a student you're expected to study throughout the bulk of the academic year, but you ramp up your revision schedule and library time during exam season. Similarly, your workload in the world of banking and finance will have a fluctuating nature about it, which is dependent on factors such as deal flow, client acquisition, quarterly reporting, market cycles, and more. Lastly, the hours in the middle and back office tend to be a little less intense and here you can expect to work anywhere from 8 am or 9 am to 6 pm in your first few years.

CHAPTER 14

CV/RÉSUMÉ

Your CV is arguably one of the most important documents you'll ever work on during your academic career, and so it's imperative to get it right. This chapter aims to help you do just that. We're going to cover the typical structure, as well as the dos and don'ts of creating a CV that stands out, gets you noticed, and takes you to the next stage of the application process, irrespective of whether that's for an interview or assessment centre, or a spring week, internship, or graduate scheme.

I've personally seen, reviewed, and worked on hundreds, if not thousands, of CVs over the last decade, and can fairly easily spot a CV that's likely to get through to the next stage, versus a CV that's likely to get the candidate rejected. If you're in need of a CV template to get started with, visit www.afzalhussein.com where you'll be able to download my recommended format. With that, let's dive in.

STRUCTURE

The typical structure of an undergraduate or postgraduate finance and banking CV has the following sections: Education, Work Experience,

Additional Experience and Positions of Responsibility, Hobbies and Interests. Let's go through each of these in turn.

Education

This section should be the first section at the top of your CV, beneath your name and email address, and you can label it Academic Experience or Educational Background. You should include academic grades such as your GCSEs (or international equivalents), A-levels (or International Baccalaureate), your degree subject, and any previously attained degrees. For each experience you want to also include their start and end dates (month/year format will suffice). Additionally, if you have completed, or are working towards completing, any finance-related certifications or qualification, such as the CFA (Chartered Financial Analyst) or any other designation that's industry-relevant, feel free to include a line on it in this section. One last point on the education section, try your best to keep it short and aim for 10–15% of your CV being spent on this first section. The aim of this section is to showcase that you're a high-achieving, academically capable individual. You don't want it to dominate your CV as interview offers aren't handed out based on academic excellence alone, employers (and employees) want to see what else you bring to the table (i.e. what you have done outside of academia).

Work Experience

This section can be titled Work Experience or Relevant Experience. Use Relevant Experience when you have two or more relevant experiences to talk about. Otherwise, stick to Work Experience. In terms of the order for listing your experiences, throughout your CV you should list experiences and achievements from most recent (at the top) to oldest (the further down the CV you go).

Additional Experience and Positions of Responsibility

This section can include any other experiences, voluntary commitments, and/or significant roles in societies or clubs. This section is of vital importance to candidates who don't have strong, if any, relevant work experience. As such, this section should focus on illustrating the initiative you've taken to actively try and learn about, and get involved in, industry-related activities. Think about it, if a CV has no finance work experience and no finance-related additional experiences such as being a member of a finance-related society at university, or taking on a leadership role in a finance-related society, the impression you'll get from reviewing the CV is that the candidate has made no effort whatsoever to learn about the industry they're supposedly interested in breaking into. Compare this with a CV that doesn't have any finance-related work experience but does have extracurricular activities related to finance. It'll be a lot easier to decide which CV gets put through to the next stage of the hiring process. Therefore, don't neglect this section of your CV.

Hobbies and Interests

Otherwise written as 'Hobbies, Interests, and Certifications' or 'Interests, Skills, and Other,' this section is typically at the bottom of your CV. If you're including any personal interests, they don't have to be finance related, although if you genuinely have a niche interest in something finance related you should most definitely include it. Other things worth adding here include any language you can fluently communicate in, your proficiency in using Microsoft Excel, PowerPoint, and Word, any useful certificates you have—whether finance or coding related (more relevant for technology and trading floor roles), listing the names of firms you've attended insight days with, and anything else that's interesting about you. Target three to four lines max on this section and be comfortable with talking about any specific interests or hobbies at length, as they can often be a topic of conversation towards the end of interviews.

KEEP IT TO ONE PAGE

At the start of your career (when you're in university, or when you're applying to entry-level roles), it's common practice to have a one-page CV. After three or so years, it's totally fine to have a longer CV. However, when it comes to spring weeks, internships, and graduate schemes in the world of banking and finance, a one-page CV is the norm. The firms you're applying to simply don't have the time to review even the one-page CV itself, let alone any additional pages. After all, investment banks receive hundreds of thousands of applications each year and the employees (often analysts, associates, and directors from the teams that are hiring, not just human resource professionals) all end up reviewing CVs on top of a long list of their own work that needs to be done. This is why it's so important to make sure your CV has the ability to grab the reader's attention in less than 20 seconds. Most CVs won't receive any more than 60–90 seconds of attention from the reviewer. As such, in order to avoid having important information missed, I encourage you to avoid submitting a CV that's longer than one page. To add to that, be sure to italicise or bolden any key achievements, awards, or certifications (don't overdo it) that you want to grab the reader's attention and ensure that your CV looks well-presented and is easy to follow.

WHAT TO DO WITH LOW GRADES

A common question I receive from applicants is, 'What should I put if I have low grades so far in my university degree?' My advice is pretty straightforward: if you've achieved low grades previously, there's no way around it and they have to be included on your CV, otherwise it'll look like you're hiding something. Analyse the average scores you've been achieving for tests or assignments and think about what you're realistically likely to be able to achieve. Put this as your predicted grade. Additionally, it's always worth remembering that your CV is a one-page pitch, and you shouldn't sell yourself short. Because if you do, someone else out there, who's less capable than you, will likely end up in an interview that you should be in because they didn't make the mistake of selling themselves short on their CV. Never lie but always remember to self-promote as best you can.

TEMPLATES AND FORMATTING

Don't worry about creating a nice CV template from scratch. You can download my Goldman Sachs CV template at www.afzalhussein.com. What's more important is drafting a clean and professional one-page CV, using either Times New Roman or Arial fonts in sizes 10, 11, or 12, in black and white, with minimal clutter. You don't need to include any head-shots or photos of your face, and you don't need to include any lines at the top of your CV that act as a Personal Profile highlighting why you're so great, motivated, and worth hiring. These personal profile blurbs add nothing to the CV and simply use up important space that you can't afford to waste.

POWERFUL BULLET POINTS

Your CV should include powerful bullet points. What's a powerful bullet point? It's a bullet point that starts with an action verb like 'managed', 'developed', 'initiated', or 'led', followed by an explanation of a situation or experience, and ending with a result achieved or skill learned. The CVs that use powerful bullet points to explain previous experiences are the CVs that tend to stand out and proceed to the next stage of the application process.

For context, here are a few examples of powerful bullet points:

- Led a team of five to organise a finance conference, resulting in a 20% increase in attendance year-over-year.
- Developed my teamwork and communication skills as a barista at Starbucks, which resulted in the fastest promotion in the store's history.
- Played a substantial role in the Economics Society's success and growth, collaborating seamlessly with team members to orchestrate successful events and initiatives that positively impacted the community, resulting in a 39% increase in event attendance.
- Achieved top academic performance by strategically prioritising and batching tasks; honed leadership capabilities by mentoring and assisting younger students.
- Applied financial modelling techniques to analyse investment opportunities for a student-run fund, achieving a 20% increase in portfolio returns.

You want to display the skills you've learned. Ideally, these will also be the key competency skills that are preferred for the role that you're applying to. A simple way to identify which key competency skills the role requires is by looking at the job description and expectations for successful candidates. Then, you simply include these buzzwords throughout your CV whilst backing them up with examples of developing them in your previous experiences.

QUANTIFYING BULLET POINTS

Creating powerful bullet points is a great starting point for any candidate who wants to immediately improve their CV. However, if you want to go one step further, you should constantly focus on quantifying your bullet points where possible. This is how the best candidates separate themselves from the hundreds of thousands of other candidates who also apply to the same roles. In order to quantify your results, you don't just say what you did, you quantify the result by using percentages, figures, statistics, and data. The world of finance and banking is all about numbers. Profits for companies, and bonuses for individuals, are all determined and measured by the results achieved. As such, your ability to show the reader (an industry professional) that you understand this expectation and are a results-driven individual will score extra points when your CV is being reviewed. As an example, instead of writing 'Worked in a retail role', it would be better to write 'Increased retail sales by 15% in six months through improved customer service and designing a loyalty programme'.

THE VALUE OF RELEVANT AND IRRELEVANT EXPERIENCE

The most valuable experience for you to include on your CV is any experience directly relevant or related to the role you're applying for. If you've worked on any interesting deals or projects related to the role or division, you should most definitely expand on these and dedicate more space on your one-page CV for this experience compared to other experiences. Writing more bullet points for the most relevant experiences is a useful use of space as it shows off and focuses on the skills required for the role and will prove interesting for the person reviewing your CV.

Relevant experience doesn't necessarily need to be in the form of paid full-time or part-time work experience. It can come in the form of extra-curricular activities, society memberships, and side projects like managing your own portfolio of investments, starting a business as a side hustle, working on a piece of coursework that contributes to the finance industry, and so on. As such, you should also dedicate more than the average amount of space for these experiences on your CV if they're directly relevant to the role you are applying to.

Next, we have irrelevant experiences. Unrelated experiences (i.e. any experience that isn't directly related to the role or industry you're applying to) are still important and useful. Why? Because at the undergraduate and entry career level you're not expected to have tons of specific and technical knowledge (although it definitely does help having it). What's more important, for most roles, is the set of soft skills that you possess. When we say soft skills, we're simply referring to key competency skills such as communication, interpersonal, time management, problem-solving, leadership, analytical thinking, attention to detail, and so on. And the great news is that these skills can all be developed in irrelevant experiences, whether it be working as a barista at a coffee shop or volunteering at a zoo. This is why it's important to leverage irrelevant experiences to highlight your relevant skills for the role, especially if you lack relevant experiences to include on your CV.

Common Mistakes to Avoid

The most common mistakes I see on CVs are around inconsistent formatting, sloppy punctuation, and poor grammar. Your CV is meant to display a high level of attention to detail, and if you can't do that, it simply tells the reader you're not ready for a role that often requires sending important documents and pieces of work to clients. Essentially, if you can't put enough time and attention into creating an error-free CV, then why should anyone invite you for an interview for a role that requires such a high level of attention to detail, on a daily basis, and where the cost of an error in a document, trade, or recommendation could cost the firm, or client, millions of dollars. Imperfect formatting, grammar, and punctuation save employees a lot of time, as nine times out of ten these CVs will be immediately rejected.

Common mistakes candidates make on their CVs include: some bullet points ending with full stops while others don't (whichever you decide on, just be consistent), spelling mistakes, margins being too close to the edge of the page or closer on one side than the other, multiple fonts being used, which can make the CV look less professional, too many mixed font sizes, and, last but not least, too much content crammed together with not enough white space between—give your CV breathing room as you want it to be easy on the eye and thus a pleasure to read. It never hurts to get someone who's already in the industry, or a friend who has secured an offer, to review your CV.

An important point worth mentioning is to never lie on your CV. You can easily be found out, and the last thing you want tied to your reputation is that you're unethical, ingenuine, and a liar. Word travels fast in this industry, and people move around from firm to firm, so it's best to be as truthful as you can in your applications and interviews.

TIPS ON TAILORING YOUR CV

While I encourage you to try your best to customise your CV for each role you apply to (where necessary), this can be time-consuming and arduous if you're applying to 30+ roles. Instead, my advice to you is to figure out one or two divisions that are most interesting and appealing to you. If you want to be tactical, you can identify a front-office division and a middle or back-office division to use as a hedge (i.e. protect yourself in case you don't secure a front-office role) and focus specifically on creating a separate CV for each of those divisions.

After all, there's no point applying to, say, the asset management division with a generic CV or one written with securing a role in the operations division in mind, and vice versa. So, take the time to craft two CVs (it'll be worth it), but keep in mind that this doesn't mean creating two brand new and separate CVs. You simply need to tailor your bullet points and/or adjust the experiences you've included in each CV, so they better suit the role or division you're applying to.

Whenever you're applying to a firm, division, or role, your main aim should be to tailor your CV as best you can in order to capture the reader's attention. Remember, the person on the other side of the screen or within the firm that reviews your application and CV is human. They'll have a bias to candidates who go above and beyond. They're more likely to put you through to the next stage of the application process if they can see that you've made an effort to actively tailor your CV and make it specific to their company, division, or role. Examples of doing this can include attending company-specific networking events and mentioning who you met and what you learned, attending insight days or evenings, mentioning relevant work experience, name-dropping employees from the division or across the firm, mentioning company-specific initiatives that you can relate to and/or have read about online, and so on.

To add to that, if you've worked on any interesting deals or anything specific to the role, expand on it as much as possible. Often, and I assume for consistency purposes, I see applicants writing the same number of bullet points for each of their experiences throughout their CV. You should avoid doing this and focus on writing more bullet points for the more relevant experiences, and fewer bullet points for the experiences that are less relevant.

NON-FINANCE CANDIDATES

If you're not studying a finance or banking-related degree, don't worry, it's not the end of the world. In fact, it could be advantageous since most, if not all, firms make an active effort to hire candidates from a range of degree disciplines outside of the traditional finance, banking, accounting, and other fields. For example, during my time at Goldman Sachs, the analyst to the right of me studied Spanish at university, and another analyst who sat behind me studied history and politics, yet there we were all doing the same work helping our clients with their investment needs. The reason I tell you this is because, for the most part, everything you need to know and do to succeed in the world of finance and banking is learnable, and most importantly, it's all mostly learned on the job. And so, if you're from a non-finance background, you're in a great position as you can easily show your initiative and interest in the industry by highlighting any qualifications, modules, or topics related to banking and finance that you've taken.

It's worth keeping in mind, however, if you are doing a finance or banking degree, that you won't get extra credit for listing finance-related modules as these are a given and expected. Instead, highlight certifications outside of your academic degree, such as the CFA (Chartered Financial Analyst), IMC (Investment Management Certificate), or Series Exams (for US-based applicants).

FINAL CHECKS

The simplest way to ensure your CV is error free is to print it out and run through it with a red pen. If you do this, I guarantee you'll spot mistakes that you didn't see on screen. Also, you should try the 30-second test with as many people as you can. The 30-second test is an easy way to find out what stands out in your CV and grabs people's attention. You simply start by asking someone you trust (ideally someone working in the industry or someone who's secured an offer) to review your CV for 30 seconds before taking it off them. And then you ask them to tell you what they recall from your CV, or what stood out the most in those short 30 seconds. Based on their response, you'll be able to tweak your CV accordingly. For example, if you wanted a certain achievement to stand out, but it didn't grab the reader's attention, you might tweak it in some way (underline, bolden, or italicise, for example). The 30-second test is important and useful as it's likely the amount of time your CV will receive when being reviewed as part of an application submission to investment banks.

It's worth mentioning that CV feedback and reviews are all subjective. As such, you should be aware that if you ask 100 people to review your CV, you'll likely receive 100 different pieces of feedback, of which many will be contradictory. So try to avoid getting too bogged down by excessive feedback. Instead, focus on finding three to five trusted individuals who themselves have strong CVs, and seek their feedback only.

EVERY LINE SERVES A PURPOSE

Every line on your CV should serve a purpose. Once you've completed your CV, go through it and for each line ask yourself: Does this line add value? If a line doesn't serve a purpose or add any value, take it out.

Put yourself in the shoes of the person reviewing your CV. Whether it's an analyst, someone from human resources, an associate, or a director at the investment bank, it's good to put yourself in their shoes. Imagine you were deciding who to put through to the interview stage of the hiring process. Would your CV impress and make it through? Be as honest and critical as you can to ensure that every line on your CV is serving a purpose and thus is there for a reason.

Another simple way to get the most out of your CV is to ask yourself 'so what?' at the end of each line. It's great for your lines to add value, but if you want to go even further, context is important. By asking yourself 'so what?', typically at the end of a powerful bullet point, you'll be prompted to strengthen the line by adding a result achieved or a skill learned. As such, doing so will ensure that value is being added throughout your CV, rather than just making random statements for the sake of it.

Summary

If, like many students and applicants, you're not one of the lucky few with loads of experience or extracurriculars to talk about, here's what you should do: focus on the experience you do have and highlight the relevant skills you've gained, even if the experience itself seems irrelevant.

For example, let's say you worked part-time as a barista. Even though it's not a financial institution and doesn't seem directly related to finance or banking, you've likely developed relevant skills including, but not limited to, customer service, client servicing, communication, teamwork, and more.

As previously mentioned, you can leverage these skills on your CV by focusing on what you learned from the role, what these skills have taught you, and the results you achieved whilst working in the role and making use of these key competency skills. For example, did you improve teamwork, increase efficiency, drive more sales, or reduce waiting times at the coffee shop? Whatever it is, you need to highlight examples that show you've developed these skills, and don't forget to quantify the results achieved where possible. This is a simple way to turn seemingly unrelated experiences into value-add contributions on your CV.

Furthermore, keep in mind that as a student or undergraduate, employers don't expect you to have a ton of relevant experience, and so employees are often forgiving, particularly if you display in other parts of your CV that you're trying to actively make an effort to learn more about the industry or are going above and beyond by pursuing qualifications, for example, in your spare time. They understand that as an early careers candidate you're still at the start of your journey. This, of course, will all depend on who reviews your CV (some employees are harsher than others), and each individual will naturally assign a different level of value to the various parts of your CV. But once again, most people can be quite lenient if you're able to show some initiative and effort in building relevant, industry-related experience or knowledge.

Lastly, and I say this at every talk I do in front of students because it's an easy win that's often disregarded by most: when joining societies and groups at university, don't just be a member. Anyone can sign up and attend events. What you want to do is try your best to take on an active leadership role. This will set you apart from everyone who's just a member of a society or group, and it'll give you more to talk about in your CV and at interviews. A leadership role or position of responsibility is much more impressive than just attending events, since it requires you to make things happen, learn and develop, and achieve results such as honing the essential skills required should you successfully break into the world of banking. So, focus on joining relevant societies and groups, and get actively involved. The sooner you do this, the better.

Visit www.afzalhussein.com for access to my free 75-minute CV mastery course.

CHAPTER 15

COVER LETTER

Your cover letter is arguably the second most important document, after your CV, that you'll work on during your academic and early career journey. It'll act as a key aid to your CV submission and plays a pivotal role in helping you go from applicant to interviewee. As such, it's imperative to focus on creating an outstanding cover letter that not only grabs the reader's attention but also creates a sense of curiosity about you in the reader, so much so that they decide to find out more about you by inviting you in for an interview. In this chapter I'll explain how the best cover letters are structured, what they include, and how they're able to stand out from the crowd so that you can take these common practices and implement them in your own cover letter for applications.

STRUCTURE

The most common cover letter structure is the three-part structure that aims to answer the following three questions across three paragraphs:

- Why do you want to work for this firm?

- Why do you want to work for this division?
- Why should we hire you?

By structuring your cover letter in this way you're essentially answering the three most important questions that the employee reading your cover letter will want to know before putting you through to the interview stage of the hiring process. Additionally, by following this structure your cover letter will have direction and avoid going off on any tangents.

With regard to including introductory and concluding paragraphs, you should include them in your cover letter for applications that request a cover letter upload. However, many applications that you complete will ask you to paste the contents of your cover letter into a box with a 300 or so word limit. In these instances, you don't need to include introductory and concluding paragraphs. You should focus only on answering the three questions mentioned above ('Why the firm?', 'Why the division?', and 'Why you?') within that 300-word limit. A roughly equal split of the 300 words across the three questions will suffice.

PERSONALISATION AND SPECIFICITY

The key to impressing any reader of your cover letter is through personalisation and specificity. What this means is making your cover letter specific to you and extremely tailored to the organisation and division that you're applying to, such that the reader immediately feels obliged to put you through to the next stage of the hiring process given the level of research you've carried out, and the level of effort you've put into writing your cover letter. Essentially, you want your cover letter to be so personalised and specific that the reader feels uncomfortable not putting you through to the next stage.

So how do you go about making your cover letter specific and personalised? It's actually pretty straightforward. The easiest way to find relevant and specific information is to explore the company's website, LinkedIn page, blog posts and articles, company podcasts (if they have any), social media, industry reports and publications, employee testimonials, company YouTube channel, recent news stories (a simple Google search on the company or division, followed by clicking on the 'News' tab), and so on.

The key areas you should focus on when doing this research are company culture, recent achievements, deals, acquisitions, milestones, earnings, strategic goals, organisational structure, the specific needs of the division you're applying to, any non-business initiatives that the firm is involved in that resonate with you, and anything else that catches your attention and seems interesting.

The more specific and tailored you can make your cover letter, the more likely it is to set you apart from other candidates and help you progress to the next stage of the hiring process. However, this doesn't mean you should go and include tons of random information about the firm or division in your cover letter. *You need to be tactical and strategic.* You should only include and mention things that you genuinely find interesting and relevant to the firm or division specifically. Don't include things you'll be unable to have a conversation about in an interview. And yes, do expect to talk about and expand on topics you've mentioned in your cover letter during interviews.

Lastly, it's important to make it a habit to ask yourself 'Why am I including this sentence in my cover letter?'. By doing so, you'll prompt yourself to avoid simply stating facts and figures about the firm (which anyone can do), and go further by adding to them and including what they mean to you and how they've helped you decide that this is the right firm, division, or role for you to work in.

Action Verbs

Similar to the bullet points in your CV, you should try to implement parts of the powerful bullet point formula into the sentences in your cover letter. For example, you should aim to include action verbs such as *led, managed, developed, improved, honed, taught, enriched, collaborated,* and so on in your sentences in order for them to carry more meaning and have a greater impact on the reader. Once again, don't just state what you did. Try to include a result that you achieved (quantify this where possible) or a skill or key competency that you developed as a result of the experience or whatever it is that you're describing or talking about.

Name-Dropping

Mentioning the names of industry professionals, particularly individuals who work at the firm that you're applying to, is a must where possible. However, only name-drop if you've genuinely met, interacted, and connected with someone such that they're comfortable being mentioned in your application. If so, then mentioning them in your cover letter is the fastest way to grab the reader's attention, show initiative, and stand out compared to other candidates. However, name-dropping is easier said than done because it means you have to actually forge a connection and attend many meetings with an industry professional. Doing so is somewhat easier for those of you in major cities like London or New York, where most firms host insight evenings and events for you to meet and network with their employees.

It's important to mention, you don't want to randomly name-drop someone for the sake of name-dropping. The person you name-drop needs to have some relevance to your cover letter, like being related to the division or role you're applying to, or sharing a unique insight or interest in a particular area of finance and banking that ties into your own interests and curiosities. As always, the more specific, the better. For example, the best name-drops are those that are role-specific, followed by division-specific, and then firm-specific. Last but not least, before you decide to name-drop any given employee, ask yourself how unique this person is, and whether other candidates will easily be able to find and name-drop this person. If lots of candidates are name-dropping the same person, mentioning this person in your cover letter may not add value.

However, what are you meant to do if you're not lucky enough to attend such events and connect with professionals in person? This is where the power of the internet and LinkedIn comes in. You essentially have two options. An easy, simple, and less impressive option (but still better than not name-dropping) and a higher-effort, harder, but more impressive option. The easy option is all about using the internet to research the firm and find specific employees who you can name-drop. The hard option is all about reaching out to professionals on LinkedIn and basically networking.

Using the Internet to Research the Firm

Every firm will have a presence online. This will range from podcasts to LinkedIn posts, and articles to YouTube videos. What you want to do is find content that is specific and relevant to the firm or division that you're applying to (role-specific is best, but harder to find), and you want to make a note on the employee's name and title. You don't want this to be the CEO, or someone too known across the industry, as doing this will be less impressive since the barrier to knowledge will be low. Try to find an employee between the associate and managing director level, as they're more likely to be known across the division or team that you're applying to.

Once you find someone who's produced, written, or spoken about a particular topic that genuinely interests you, search their name across the internet (LinkedIn, YouTube, company website, Google, Google 'News', etc.) and consume as much of their content as you can. You want to build a picture of this person who specialises in a particular sector, industry, or asset class. This is important and meaningful as they're someone diving deep into an area of interest to you. As such, they're highly relevant and it makes a lot of sense to name-drop them in your cover letter, mentioning what you've learned from them or highlighting a viewpoint of theirs and how you find it interesting, or how it ties into your broader interests around the topic.

Reaching Out to Professionals on LinkedIn

To leverage LinkedIn is to play the long game. This is something I probably should have done a lot more of when I was in your shoes. Then again, back then LinkedIn wasn't as popular as it is today, and doing such a thing, as an introvert, would have been so far out of my comfort zone that I'd probably have kept putting it off. However, now more than ever, leveraging LinkedIn can be a powerful tool in your search to break into the industry. There are a few ways of going about it that can maximise your chances of actually getting responses from professionals, and subsequently securing meetings and building relationships with them.

There are three things to keep in mind. First is the type of person you reach out to. Second is the length of your message. Third is the ask or request itself.

The type of person you reach out to will heavily impact the number of responses you receive. What you want to do is reach out to individuals ideally one to three years ahead of you in their career. Why? Because these individuals are most likely to reply, will feel a greater sense of connection and relatability, and will be most likely to know how it feels to be in your shoes (since it wasn't all that long ago). Then, you want to start with individuals who share a common connection or interest with you. For example, you're more likely to hear back from a school, college, or university alumni, or someone who's part of a niche community or group that you're also a part of, compared to someone who isn't either of these things. When you reach out to people who have some pre-existing mutual connection or interest, they're more likely to feel inclined to respond, since they'll connect with and relate to you a lot more than if a random student or graduate reached out to them.

Next, you want to keep your message concise. Industry professionals rarely check their LinkedIn messages, so on the off chance that they do you need to get your message across in as effective a way as possible. These individuals don't have time to read an essay about you. A simple three- to five-sentence message with an intriguing subject line is all you need. For example, when thinking about the subject line don't make it too generic like 'Requesting 30 Minutes of Your Time' or 'Can I Buy You a Coffee?'. Instead, pique their interest by mentioning the mutual tie by having the subject read something like '15 Minutes for XYZ University Student' or 'Quick Question from XYZ Society Member', where XYZ is a university, society, or other mutually connected group you both attend/ed.

Last but not least, in terms of the content of your message, make sure to briefly introduce yourself, what you're studying and/or your current situation, your career aspirations in the form of a one-sentence current goal, and what you'd like from the person you're messaging.

Here's an example:

Hi Afzal, I hope you're doing well and apologies for messaging you out of the blue. I'm a second-year Econ student at QM with a keen interest in breaking into asset management, more specifically on the institutional sales side, and was wondering if you might have 15 minutes in the next few weeks for a brief call? I am flexible and can work around your schedule. Thanks for reading my message. Best, XYZ.

If you're a half-decent human being, working in the industry, without hundreds of these messages already in your inbox, or any free time whatsoever in the coming weeks, it'd be pretty hard to say 'no' and turn down a request like this. Why? Well, I've written the message in a way that shows a high level of specificity and research (I don't just say asset management, I mention a specific role/team), respect for the person's time (all I ask for is 15 minutes as opposed to 30 minutes or more), thoughtfulness (I mention I'm happy to work around their schedule), time consciousness (I know they're busy, so I let them know any time they can carve out would be greatly appreciated), and good manners (I thank them for taking the time to read my message). These are the small things that make a big difference. However, don't feel disheartened if you don't receive as many replies as you might have expected. The truth is, people are busy, have lives outside of work, and don't owe you anything.

As illustrated in my message above, when you're reaching out to industry professionals, I'd recommend asking for 15 minutes of their time over a video call at a time and date that's suitable for them, and stress that you can be extremely flexible and work around their schedule. By doing these two very subtle things, you're telling them that you appreciate and respect their time (hence you're asking for 15 minutes as opposed to 30 minutes like everyone else does), and you understand that they're doing you a favour if they give you their time (hence you're willing to be flexible and work around their schedule). It's these subtleties that make individuals stand out and get responses when cold messaging people. Too often I see students do the opposite. I receive emails and LinkedIn messages all the time asking for 30 minutes, sometimes even an hour of my time, to help the candidate with a list of their current dilemmas and challenges, no mention or effort made in showing respect for my time or offering to be of value to me, and the tone usually comes across as extremely entitled. This approach is the fastest way to get ignored, blocked, or remembered for all the wrong reasons. Avoid such an approach at all costs.

Once you've been able to successfully secure a 15-minute call with someone working in the industry, the next step is to join the call prepared with two to four solid questions (i.e. not questions that you could find the answers to with a quick Google or ChatGPT search). Focus on getting the individual to do most of the talking by asking them questions about their experience breaking into the industry, the culture of the firm and division they're working in, anything specific about their role, and advice for you given your current situation.

At the back of your mind, be sure to think of ways in which you can name-drop them in your cover letter in a way that flows well with the rest of it. But be sure to ask them for their approval and show them the sentence you hope to include about them in your cover letter before you go ahead and include it.

A good hack to secure a second meeting with them is to ask them what specific thing they would advise you to do over the next four weeks given your current situation. Once you do whatever it is they mentioned, it'll be an excellent excuse to set up another call with them 'to provide an update on progress'. Make sure you've made enough progress to exceed their expectations as you don't want to waste their time, and don't just provide an update but be sure to go into the meeting with well-thought-out questions and, if possible, a way of adding value for them (this could be in the form of some research, sharing a useful resource, bringing good points and research to the call, or just entertaining the conversation in a valuable way).

The more meetings and calls you have with industry professionals, the better you'll get at them, you'll grow your confidence and your network, you'll nurture strong relationships, and you'll be more likely to name-drop in your cover letter.

Summary

The LinkedIn method for name-dropping requires more effort carrying out research online. However, the reward for successfully using this method to name-drop in your cover letter is the most impressive. How? Well, it's better to be able to say 'Having spoken to/met with X' or 'Being mentored by X' than it is to say 'Having read a research report by X/watched an interview with X'. These are small nuances, but they make a big difference. Think of it like this, if you're reading through hundreds of candidate cover letters, aside from good grades and strong work experience, what would grab your attention and make you put a candidate through to the next stage of the hiring process? For most people it'll be a combination of being able to tell that the candidate has gone above and beyond in order to make their cover letter specific to the firm, division, and role, and that the candidate has put in lots of time and effort beyond what the average candidate would to be able to do so. Ideally, you want to be that candidate. You want your cover letter to display so much specificity and effort that the reader feels like they're making their firm miss out on someone of high potential by not putting you through to the next round. If you're lucky enough to have industry connections, be sure to leverage them.

COMMON MISTAKES

Some of the most common mistakes I see in cover letters include poor structure and formatting, too much content, which can overwhelm the reader, and a lack of specificity. Let's address each of these individually.

Firstly, the simplest way to avoid poor structuring when it comes to your cover letter is to follow the three- or five-paragraph framework.

Three-paragraph framework (300 words, if you copy and paste into the application):

- First paragraph: Why do you want to work for this firm?
- Second paragraph: Why the division?
- Third paragraph: Why are you the best candidate?

Five-paragraph framework (400–500 words, if you upload a pdf of your cover letter):

- Introduction
- Second paragraph: Why do you want to work for this firm?
- Third paragraph: Why the division?
- Fourth paragraph: Why are you the best candidate?
- Conclusion

Remember, most people reviewing your cover letter don't have the time or patience to read the entire page. After the initial screening that the human resources team does, your cover letter will be reviewed by analysts, associates, and directors in the teams that are hiring, and these individuals have tons of work of their own that needs attending to as opposed to sitting and reading through candidate cover letters. As such, you have around 30 seconds to grab and hold their attention. So the last thing you want to do is overwhelm them in the first instance by writing in a long-winded and poorly organised way. It's common practice to aim to keep your cover letter to between 60% and 75% of a page (which is around 300–400 words).

Last but not least, you don't want the reader of your cover letter to be able to change the name of the firm within your cover letter to a different firm and the cover letter still reads effectively and makes sense. If they can, it means your cover letter is too generic and you haven't carried out the level of research and due diligence into the firm, division, or role in order to stand out, let alone compete with the highest calibre of candidates you'll be up against. A simple way to fix this is to constantly ask yourself 'Is this sentence applicable only to this firm?' for sentences within the 'Why this company?' and 'Why this division?' paragraphs. For the most part, if the answer is 'yes' then keep it. If the answer is 'no' then consider making it more relevant.

KEY COMPETENCIES

Throughout your cover letter, be sure to include buzzwords and phrases that readers will be on the lookout for. These key competencies can be found in the roles description and typically include skills such as time management, analytical skills, interpersonal skills, teamwork, communication, attention to detail, leadership, resilience, organisation, problem-solving, and so on. Oftentimes candidate applications are put through an ATS (Applicant Tracking System), which helps companies speed up the application review and general hiring process by reviewing CVs and cover letters at scale. These tracking systems tend to search for key buzzwords and phrases like the ones mentioned above, and so I'd highly recommend you leverage the job description when looking for key competencies to mention in your cover letter (and CV).

REVIEW

Once you've had a first stab at writing your cover letter be sure to print it out and review it in hand with a red pen—two simple steps that 9 times out of 10 reveal a mistake or error that requires attention. Once you've done this, try to find three to five people to review your cover letter (ideally industry professionals or peers who have successfully secured interviews and offers). When you've found people to review your cover letter, ask them to look at your cover letter for 30 seconds and then recall what parts of the cover letter stood out to them. Doing so will give you clarity on the things that need to be taken out and how better to structure the content within your cover letter.

Summary

If you do everything discussed in this chapter, I'm confident that you'll have a cover letter that's better than most other candidates' cover letters. Getting there, however, is quite an arduous and lengthy process, but once you have a strong base to work with, all you need to do is tweak the firm-specific information to each company that you apply to. Yes, it's a lot of work, especially when you're applying to so many different companies (my Excel tracker when I was in university had around 40 companies that I needed to apply to); however, it honestly makes all the difference. If you're not willing to customise your cover letter for each firm that you apply to, don't waste your time applying to that company. That's how high the standard is these days. This isn't to say that it's impossible for you to break in. You just need to carve out a strategy and plan that will enable you to put in enough hours to build a competitive advantage around your knowledge on the areas in which you're interested in pursuing a career, and master your application and interview approach along the way.

Whenever you're ready to start working on your cover letter, be sure to leverage my free 85-minute cover letter video course at www.afzalhussein.com.

CHAPTER 16

MOTIVATIONAL QUESTIONS

M otivational questions are often the make-or-break moment in any finance or banking application. These tend to come up in applications for investment banks that want to learn a little about your drive and reasons for applying before inviting you to do an online assessment or HireVue interview. They're also a useful section of your application for employees to refer to if they're struggling to decide between two candidates.

While technical skills and industry knowledge are important, recruiters want to see that you genuinely understand and are passionate about the role you're applying for. These questions are designed to uncover your motivations and often aim to find out the reasoning behind why you're applying to a specific role, firm, or the industry in general.

Answering motivational questions effectively means going beyond surface-level responses. As a general rule of thumb, the more specific, the better. I mention this every so often to members of my free online community that helps students and graduates break into the industry (visit www.afzalhussein.com for more details). Saying you want to work at Goldman Sachs because it's a 'prestigious firm' is too generic and uninspiring. Instead, dig deeper. What specifically attracts you to this firm? Is it their market-leading position in M&A? Their innovative approach to ESG? Or their reputation for developing junior talent? Tailor your answers by doing your homework on the company's culture, values, and recent achievements. If you want to go even further, simply tie your responses to your own personal journey, stories, and experiences.

For the 'Why this role?' question, focus on what excites you about the work itself. For example, if you're applying to a sales and trading role, highlight your interest in fast-paced environments and your ability to make quick decisions under pressure. If you can, name-drop someone you've networked and connected with, and what they've taught you about the role that's unique specifically to the firm. If it's investment banking, discuss your passion for deal-making, problem-solving, and working on high-impact transactions. Always include statistics and figures where possible. Quantifying examples allows you to stand out further, as opposed to simply making a surface-level statement.

Lastly, when addressing 'Why finance or banking?', bring it back to your personal story. What was the pivotal moment that changed everything for you and made you realise this is the industry and role, or firm, you want to build a career in? Maybe it was an internship or a university project that sparked your interest. Or perhaps it's your love for analytical challenges and working in a high-stakes environment. The key here is to make your answers authentic and relatable. By doing so, you'll naturally increase the potential buy-in that the reader has into your story. If you do it well enough, you'll have them rooting for you, on your side, and ready to play a key role in your success.

Remember, motivational questions aren't just about showing you're a good fit. They're about demonstrating that you've thought carefully about your career choices and are fully committed to excelling in the role. They're called 'motivational' questions for a reason. They aim to find out what's actually driving and motivating you to fill in the application form. It's okay if earning a high salary is a part of your answer (avoid mentioning this in the form just to be safe), but what else makes such a career prospect exciting for you? Dig deep into your intrinsic motivations and before you know it, you'll have crafted a few compelling answers.

CHAPTER 17

PSYCHOMETRIC TESTS

You can be the most likeable, technically gifted, behaviourally appropriate, academically capable, and financially experienced candidate to apply to investment banks, but if you don't pass the online psychometric tests, nothing else matters. Once your applications (motivational questions, CV or résumé, and cover letter) have been reviewed and approved, you'll be invited to do a few online tests (the most common are numerical reasoning, verbal reasoning, and logical reasoning). Psychometric tests are a key hurdle in most finance and banking application processes, and your ability to succeed in them can determine whether you progress to the next stage. In order to be invited for an online or in-person interview, you'll need to pass these tests. And the only way to do so is to practise as frequently and as many tests as you can possibly get your hands on. Unfortunately, there's no other way about it.

Numerical reasoning tests evaluate your ability to work with data, charts, and percentages, which are essential for roles that require analysing financial information. *Verbal reasoning* tests assess your ability to interpret written information, a critical skill for roles like investment banking or asset management, where understanding reports and industry news is crucial. And *logical reasoning* tests focus on your problem-solving and pattern-recognition abilities.

Once again, the key to acing these is all about practice. Preparation in advance is key to performing well. My advice here would be to start by familiarising yourself with the test format and timing. They're typically multiple-choice format and time-pressured, so you'll need to balance speed and accuracy without second-guessing your decisions. You can find tons of practice mock tests online with a quick Google or ChatGPT search for 'Practice Online Psychometric Tests'. When doing your research, you'll come across plenty of online resources offering free and paid practice materials. Whichever you choose to do, do a lot of them.

Another piece of advice worth mentioning is trying to develop the ability to stay calm under pressure, which I know is often easier said than done. These tests are designed to challenge you, but panicking or rushing can lead to careless mistakes. Read each question carefully, manage your time effectively, and don't dwell too long on any single question. It's better to make an educated guess and move on. You want to get to a stage where doing these tests feel like second nature. And the best way to get there is to do as many of them as possible such that the format, question styles, and scenarios are nothing you haven't already come across and learned the appropriate way to answer.

It's also worth mentioning that the pass mark (you'll usually have 20 questions to answer in around 16–18 minutes) can vary from division to division. What I mean by this is that the score required to pass psychometric tests (or the questions themselves) for investment banking, sales and trading, or other front-office divisions will typically be higher (or more difficult) than the pass mark (or questions) for back-office divisions.

This is something worth considering when being strategic about securing an offer and getting your foot in the door.

Lastly, while psychometric tests might seem like a box-ticking exercise, they're actually a key way to prove your analytical and problem-solving skills. Take them seriously (don't try and get someone else to do them for you as you'll often be asked to resit them in person when invited to an assessment centre), prepare diligently, and you'll have a strong chance of standing out from the competition.

CHAPTER 18

ASSESSMENT CENTRES

Assessment centres are often the final hurdle in the finance and banking recruitment process. They're intense, full-day or half-day, multi faceted evaluations designed to test not just your technical abilities but also your teamwork, communication, and problem-solving skills. Think of them as a simulation of the real-world challenges you'd face in the role.

Assessment centres include a mix of activities including group exercises where you'll need to collaborate with other candidates to solve a division-specific business problem or case study, psychometric tests, group presentations, individual presentations, networking with employees, role play, and interviews.

Throughout an assessment centre, recruiters are watching how you interact with others. They'll be keeping an eye out on whether you're a leader, a good listener, a team player, or someone who bulldozes through discussions and disregards what other people have to say. Striking the right balance between assertiveness and collaboration is key, whilst also being good at bringing useful ideas and opinions to the table. If you notice one of the candidates is being ignored or they're generally introverted and quiet, try to bring them into the discussion. This shows you're aware of others and are an encouraging team member. Although offers will be handed out individually, it's better to display the traits of a strong team player who has the ability to build relationships with others, as opposed to going about things as a lone ranger.

In terms of case studies, you'll be given a real-world business scenario (typically an actual client case study from a while ago) and asked to analyse data, identify issues, and propose solutions. This is your chance to showcase your analytical thinking and commercial awareness. You'll typically have tons of resources and materials to examine, but very little time to examine them all. As such, you'll need to prioritise the key problem at hand and identify the relevant information from all of the data in order to make a suitable recommendation or proposal for a solution. Always remember to structure your arguments clearly and back them up with evidence—there's no point saying something and then not being able to back it up. These case studies will rarely be made up, and so when the case study exercise has ended, it's an easy conversation starter or potential question to ask how the firm solved that particular case study, or how they provided a solution to the client.

Whenever you prepare for an assessment centre, be sure to also prepare for potentially the most important part of the assessment centre, the interview or interviews. These can range from competency-based interviews to technical or informal conversations with managing directors or other senior folk. It's also a good idea to prepare for brain-teaser questions, particularly if you're interviewing for front-office roles.

One of the most underestimated parts of assessment centres, which isn't formally assessed or marked, is the informal networking that'll be happening throughout the day. These networking sessions can happen over breakfast or lunch, or in between sessions. Although these breaks aren't assessed, it's important to know that they can play a huge part in your evaluation and whether you receive an offer or not. How? Well, the employees you meet and speak to during these informal networking sessions will give feedback to the human resources or recruitment team if any of the candidates in particular stood out to them. If I was an employee networking with candidates at an assessment centre lunch and network session, I'd be most impressed by any candidate who could hold a good conversation with me about their interests in the business, and anyone who had questions that were more thoughtful than the generic list of questions one might expect. This, of course, is easier said than done, and it's important to remember to simply be yourself, be enthusiastic, and show a level of curiosity that makes people feel like you're intrigued and interested by the field and potential career prospects of joining such a firm, division, or team. And it goes without saying, throughout the assessment centre you should always remain professional and engaged, no matter who you're talking to.

CHAPTER 19

INTERVIEWS

Interviews are make or break. Outperforming in interviews pretty much guarantees you a role in the world of finance and banking. However, they're arguably the toughest part of the hiring process for candidates and, as such, they require a ton of preparation and practice beforehand. The good news is that, like almost anything, interview technique can be learned. The bad news is that it can take a lot of time, effort, failure, and rejection in order to master it.

When it comes to interview preparation, there's quite a lot that you need to consider ahead of time. At the most basic level, you should always take a notepad and pen to any interview, whilst being dressed not to stand out, but to fit in. You can't go wrong with a dark navy suit, white shirt, and a simple patterned or plain tie, if you're a guy. For the women, I'm no expert but my advice would be to also aim for a classy look, leveraging dark colours and making sure to wear a pair of heels that you're comfortable walking in, if you decide to wear heels. Once again, the goal here is to blend in unnoticed, rather than stand out.

Aside from what to wear to an interview, there's tons of preparation tips and techniques worth considering. In this chapter I'll cover everything you need to know ahead of your interview, so you know exactly what to expect and how best to approach it when the time comes.

The topics covered in this chapter include competency and behavioural interviews (including the STAR technique to answer competency and behavioural interview questions), technical interviews, brain teasers, online (HireVue) interviews, telephone interviews, in-person interviews, final-round interviews, and questions to ask the interviewer.

COMPETENCY AND BEHAVIOURAL INTERVIEWS

Competency and behavioural interviews are very similar in that their main focus is on assessing the key competency skills (attention to detail, teamwork, communication and interpersonal skills, time management, leadership capabilities, problem-solving abilities, analytical nature, etc.) of candidates by learning about their past experiences and behaviours as a barometer for suitability and future performance.

Competency and behavioural interviews focus on identifying whether a candidate has the relevant soft skills and personality traits required for the role, whereas technical interviews focus on the hard skills (technical capabilities, knowledge, and insight). Here are five examples of common competency and behavioural interview questions:

- Describe a situation where you led a team or supported a struggling team member.
- What was the last big decision you had to make and how did you decide which option to choose?

- Give an example of when you had to work with someone who was difficult to get along with. How did you handle interactions with that person?
- Describe a time when you had to persuade a co-worker or manager.
- Tell me about a time you made a mistake. How did you handle the situation?

Now that you know what to expect from competency and behavioural-style interviews, let's dive into how best to structure your responses to successfully answer such questions.

STAR Technique

The STAR (Situation, Task, Action, Result) technique is a commonly used framework for answering competency and behavioural interview questions, and for good reason. It's simple to understand, straightforward to implement, easy to remember, and effective in creating solid answers. However, it does require practice and some getting used to. Let's run through how it works.

The way I like to prepare for competency and behavioural interviews is to first create a list of 10–20 of the most common key competency skills that are required in the world of banking and finance, and then pinpoint three to five specific previous experiences (work experience, academic experience, extracurricular activities, volunteering, etc.) that will be the bedrock of my answers going forward. And then it's all about finding as many examples of how I specifically displayed the ability to develop or improve any given key competency skill from the long list of most common competencies within each of my previous experiences. Once I've done this in thorough detail, it allows me to feel confident that I have the data or artillery to answer any key competency or behavioural interview question.

The next step in the process is all about forming coherent answers for each competency skill using the STAR technique. Keep in mind, it's totally fine to use one previous experience as an example to describe how you developed more than one key competency skill. To begin with, let's explore what each part of the STAR technique means and requires you to do.

- *Situation.* What's the context and what previous experience are you going to be using to answer the question? What was the situation?
- *Task.* What was the task at hand that needed to be addressed or solved for? Why is it important? How does it relate to the situation?
- *Action.* What was the specific action that you took or enabled in order to move forward and progress/develop/solve the problem? Why did you take this specific action?
- *Result.* What was the outcome of your action? What results were you able to achieve? What lessons did you learn? What skills did you develop or improve?

Rest assured you don't need to answer every single one of these questions to create an answer in the STAR technique format. The above are just guiding questions for each part of the STAR technique framework. However, having the answers to all of the above questions is definitely an exercise worth spending the time doing.

Once you have a STAR framework answer for each of your 10–20 key competency skills (using three to five experiences, or more) it's time to start practising delivery of your answers. My advice here would be to avoid scripting paragraphs for each STAR answer. Instead, what you want to do for each question or competency skill is list one or two bullet points for each situation, task, action, and result related to the experience you're using to answer the question. You want to use these bullet points to guide and direct your answers in an effort to avoid sounding overly scripted. Next, you want to get as much practice in front of a mirror as possible, and have yourself video recorded. Practice makes perfect. Honestly, as with many things, most of this is simply a numbers game. If you practise each response five times, and I practise each response 500 times, who do you think is more likely to outperform in the interview? The more 'reps' you put in, the more growth and development you'll get out. And this is the only thing that stands in the way of you and an offer.

I want to stress the importance of mastering the STAR technique. Without this technique you are more likely to answer interview questions in an unstructured format. You will come across as unprepared, and you run the risk of going off on a tangent. Aim for one to two-minute responses to questions, but keep an eye on how engaged the interviewer is. You don't want to bore them by going on for ages, but you want to give enough context and meaning to your answer such that it justifies how you achieved a certain result or developed the competency skill in question.

TECHNICAL INTERVIEWS

For undergraduate and graduate positions at financial institutions you can expect generic interviews that consist of mostly competency and behavioural questions. Technical interview questions typically make up a small percentage of interviews at this level. However, for experienced professionals, and in particular for technical roles, you can expect the technical proportion of interview questions to increase. In many cases, there'll be a separate standalone technical interview in addition to any competency and behavioural interviews.

You can expect technical interview questions to broadly focus on two key areas: industry insight and division-specific knowledge. When we talk about industry insight, we're focusing on your knowledge of everything going on in the industry from a commercial awareness perspective. For example, a candidate with strong industry insight is someone who keeps up-to-date on the latest news, trends, deals, and developments that are most relevant to the division they're applying to. The more specific your knowledge, the better. But it's also good to know what's going on from a macroeconomic perspective too. You don't want to simply read articles, news stories, and recent developments for the sake of it. Instead, what sets the best candidates apart is their ability to form an opinion on the information they're consuming and thus increase their chances of having meaningful conversations about a relevant topic in interviews. When I was in university, I used to open the *Financial Times* website (it's worth checking with your university if they offer free access to the FT) and read random articles about random topics which didn't make much sense to me at the time. It was only when I started reading topics of genuine interest to me in the FTfm (Financial Times Fund Management) section that they began to develop my curiosity, lead me to carry out my own further research, understand the topics better, and form my own opinions. This newfound interest and insight were noticed in interviews.

It's also worth mentioning that each *Financial Times* article also has a comments section at the bottom. The comments section is usually filled with tons of different opinions and conversations amongst readers from different sectors, generations, industries, companies, and countries. It can be a goldmine for learning about different opinions and arguments for and against the topics being discussed. As such, I'd highly recommend you spend some time in the comments section reading through the opinions shared on the articles you end up reading. Don't just read them, however. Ask yourself whether you agree, disagree, or struggle to form an opinion. After doing so, ask yourself 'Why?'. Try to go three to five 'Why?' layers deep and before you know it, you'll be a pro at forming your own detailed opinions and viewpoints on industry-specific topics. Trust me, start reading articles on topics of interest to you (aim for one article a day) and everything else will fall into place, and feel less like a chore.

As well as commercial awareness and industry insights, if you want to maximise your chances of breaking into the industry, especially into the front office of an investment bank, you need to have division-specific technical knowledge. The exact type of knowledge here will vary from division to division, and it can be learned in a number of different ways. However, the more you understand and display the ability to understand, hone, and master the technical nature of these and other hard skills, the better you'll be positioned to break in.

If you're interested in applying to the investment banking division, the range of technical skills you'll need to break in will include, but not be limited to, being able to build complex financial models for valuation purposes using Microsoft Excel, understanding how mergers and acquisitions, capital raising, and so on all work, understanding how to make sense of a company by analysing its various financial statements, and more.

For sales and trading (global markets) candidates, you'll need to know your technical knowledge, more specifically around financial markets. For example, you'll want to be well-read and able to form opinions on how recent news stories across the world of politics, geopolitics, and beyond are impacting financial markets, and how monetary and fiscal policy changes are impacting different asset classes, countries, markets, and securities.

For asset management and private wealth management, similar to sales and trading candidates you'll want to keep abreast of what's going on in the world of financial markets, but you'll also want to have an idea and understanding of what could be at the forefront of asset management or wealth management clients' minds regarding any particular areas of finance, market movements, opportunities, threats, and so on. Furthermore, if you're particularly interested in portfolio management, for example, then it would make sense to learn about the technical nature of the portfolio management role and the various technicalities and skills required to secure and develop in such a role.

Try to stay informed and up-to-date on recent developments in the regulatory spaces for the respective divisions mentioned above, as well as the industry as a whole. After all, regulation is a key component of the industry and whenever it changes or is amended it tends to have a huge impact on some of the biggest incumbents in the industry.

For the most part there are essentially four ways that you can start to increase your technical knowledge and become an expert on the technical front for any division. Let's go through them one by one.

The first is to simply learn for free by researching the internet in order to read relevant articles and watch relevant YouTube videos. This can be quite a scattered and time-consuming approach, but rest assured everything you need to break into the industry is available online—you just need to find it and dedicate the time to learning about it in detail.

The second option you have is to leverage the use of artificial intelligence tools like ChatGPT to teach you everything you want to learn about the industry. Honestly, if you get good at using these tools and prompting them in the right way, they're complete game changers.

They'll never be as good as a mentor who has industry experience and is able to share their own unique networks, tips, and tricks to help you break in, but they do come close so be sure to use them as best as you can. Unfortunately, when I was in your shoes, I didn't have tools like ChatGPT. And if I had, I would have used them to speed up my learning about the various divisions, roles, career paths, and so on. As such, I'd highly recommend considering using artificial intelligence to aid your preparation and help you develop your technical knowledge and subject matter expertise before applying to firms across the world of finance and banking.

The third option is to learn by doing. I've known people to skip interviews for roles they're not interested in, or firms that are a lot smaller. But interview practice is so important and the more you can get, the better. A good example of learning by doing would be to practise trading by actually trading in real life using a demo or paid account if you were interested in trading roles. Doing so will enable you to learn about investing and trading, understand asset classes and financial securities, form your own opinions and preferences for trading financial instruments, and overall learn about the roles and responsibilities that come with trading. If you've been successful in trading over a certain period of time, great. It's something you can talk about in interviews and share how you've done so. If you've been trading but not so successfully, that's okay too. You'll be able to talk about what you've learned and why you think things turned out as they did, and what you'd do differently moving forward. The act of actually doing the thing, in this case trading, forms a strong case for your interest in applying to a trading role. Another example would be where a candidate is actively building financial models for valuing companies because they find it interesting and are considering a career in the investment banking division. Producing numerous financial models for different organisations will allow you to talk about your thinking and approach to doing so in interviews and applications. These are the small things that set candidates apart and hone their technical expertise over time.

Last but not least, you can learn and develop your technical skills by paying for online courses and programmes. These can range from self-paced online courses to cohort-based courses and four-week intensive programmes to longer-term mentorship schemes. Paying for structured knowledge definitely speeds up the learning process as you don't need to worry about not knowing what you don't know. So these are great options to consider given their thorough and organised format. However, the downside is that they can be quite expensive and often price out most individuals interested in breaking into the industry.

BRAIN TEASERS

Brain teasers can be some of the trickiest and most daunting interview questions out there. What's worse is facing one of these questions without ever having heard of, or expected, such a question to come up in an interview. They're purposefully random, aimed to make you think outside of the box, test how you perform under pressure, and try to gauge your intuition and thought process. Before I go through some examples, it's worth noting that brain teaser interview questions are more commonly asked in interviews for front-office roles, most commonly for the sales and trading division. However, that isn't to say that you won't get any brain teasers if you're interviewing for middle and back-office roles. Therefore, it's important to be aware of what they look like, how to prepare for them, and what the interviewer expects from you when answering such questions. Here are a few examples of common brain teaser interview questions.

You have two ropes. Each rope takes exactly one hour to burn from one end to the other. However, the ropes burn at inconsistent rates. How do you measure exactly 45 minutes?

When approaching this type of question it's important to try your best to think outside of the box. At first glance, it might seem quite a tricky challenge to solve. However, the answer is pretty straightforward once you understand the logic behind it. Although the ropes don't burn at a constant rate, we can still measure their burning patterns. A viable answer to this question would be to light the first rope at both ends whilst also lighting the second rope at one end, at the same time. The first rope will take 30 minutes to burn completely since it's burning from both ends. As soon as the first rope is fully burnt (i.e. after 30 minutes), light the other end of the second rope. Since the second rope has 30 minutes left to burn, lighting both ends will make it burn in half the time (i.e. 15 minutes). This gives you a total of 45 minutes.

There are eight identical-looking balls. One of them is slightly heavier, but you don't know which. You have a balance scale. What is the minimum number of weighings required to find the heavier ball?

It's extremely common to want to divide the balls into two groups when approaching this problem. However, this will result in three uses of the weighing scale (weighing two groups of 4, discarding one group of 4, then splitting the remaining four balls into two groups of 2, weighing these two groups, discarding one group of 2, and then finally weighing the last two balls to identify which ball is heavier). In contrast, the better approach would be to use the divide-and-conquer method to solve this in two weighings as opposed to three. For the first weighing we would divide the eight balls into three groups (two groups of 3 and one group of 2). Next, we'd weigh the two groups of three balls against each other. If one group is heavier, the heavy ball is in that group. If they balance, the heavier ball is in the remaining group of two balls. For the second and final weighing, if one group of three balls was heavier, take that group and weigh two balls against each other. If one is heavier, you've found the heavy ball. If they balance, the third ball is the heavy one. If the first weighing found that the heavy ball was in the group of 2, simply weigh those two balls against each other to find the heavier one. So the minimum number of weighings required is two.

How many light bulbs are there in the UK?

This is a classic estimation question where you're required to make some educated guesses and assumptions. The key here is to break the problem down into logical steps and show a clear thought process, rather than finding the exact number. I'd highly recommend thinking out loud in interviews when answering brain teasers, particularly like this one, as you'll show the interviewer how your mind works and that your logical thinking is able to intuitively guide you to the right answer. Here's how to answer this question.

First, you want to estimate the population of the UK, which is around 70 million people. Next, you want to estimate the number of households. A simple way to do this is to assume there are, on average, three people per household, which means in the UK there'll be roughly 70 million people divided by three people per household = 23 million households. We can then estimate that there are probably 10 rooms and hallways in the average household, with each room having at least one light bulb. Some rooms, however, might have multiple bulbs (e.g. kitchens, living rooms, hallways).

With this information we can estimate that the average number of light bulbs per household is around 15. Next, we want to estimate non-residential light bulbs, so we have to think about things like commercial buildings, offices, schools, factories, and so on. Assume that for every household, there are an additional five light bulbs in non-residential settings (offices, public buildings, streetlights, etc.). Then we can calculate the total number of light bulbs in the UK as follows: $(15 \times 23$ million$) + (5 \times 23$ million$) = 460$ million light bulbs in the UK. This is, of course, an estimation, but the interviewer just wants to see your ability to think on the spot, work under pressure, tackle a problem in an intuitive and rational way, and think logically. It's worth noting that I used simple and round numbers in order to make the calculations easier to do. You won't have a calculator in the interview so don't overcomplicate things by using complex or decimal numbers. After all, you're being assessed on your thought process rather than your mathematical acumen.

To wrap up this section on brain teasers, my advice would be to Google search or use ChatGPT to find as many example investment bank brain teaser questions and answers as possible and try to solve them on your own by thinking outside of the box, and maintaining a rational approach with an intuitive, step-by-step thought process. If you're like me, it might help to answer these questions out loud (and it's also good practice for interviews). Then, explore the answers for each question and try to prime your mind to think in such a way. Brain teasers can, and should, seem daunting at first. However, the more questions you see, attempt, and learn the solutions to, the easier they'll become.

ONLINE (HIREVUE) INTERVIEWS

There used to be a time when you would only be expected to participate in telephone interviews before being invited into assessment centres or in-person interviews. However, over the last decade or so, firms have realised that it's a lot more cost-effective and workforce-efficient to have candidates interview online without taking up the time of employees. It also means that companies are now able to 'interview' more individuals and therefore explore a broader range of applications.

Online interviews have become synonymous with HireVue interviews (HireVue have essentially cornered the market for online interviews and become the vendor of choice for hosting online interviews for pretty much every investment bank and financial institution that expects candidates to do these online interviews). Online (HireVue) interviews are most commonly 30-minute interviews where you're expected to answer anywhere from five to eight questions that appear on screen. Each question will appear for around 30 seconds and then you'll be prompted to record your answer, which will be limited to one, sometimes two, minutes. Some firms let candidates re-record their answers if they're unhappy with them. However, other firms only give you one shot at answering each question.

In terms of what types of questions you can expect, for the most part HireVue interviews predominantly focus on competency and behavioural interview questions. However, it's not uncommon for there to be at least one technical question in your interview, either related to financial markets or the specific division you're applying to.

The best way to prepare for these interviews is to prepare for them just as if you were preparing for an in-person interview. This means doing your research and creating one-pagers on the firm, the division, why they should hire you, commercial awareness, technical knowledge related to the division, and potential questions to ask. By preparing for online interviews in as much detail as you would an in-person interview you're not only setting yourself up for success, but the employees who review your video interview recording will notice the effort. Other things worth doing for all online interviews is to dress professionally, just as you would for an in-person interview; make sure everyone in the household or apartment, or wherever you're hoping to do the interview, is aware of the time and length of the interview so as to avoid any interruptions or distractions; ensure your laptop and/or earphones are fully charged, and keep a pen and paper or notes tab open in case the need arises. Lastly, it's always a good idea to have a bottle or glass of water nearby—if you need to calm yourself down, slow down the pace of your responses, or take a pause and buy yourself some time, taking a sip of water will enable you to do that.

As with anything, practice makes perfect, so I'd encourage you to get in as much real-life practice as possible by doing mock interviews with friends or peers as well as answering questions to the camera of your screen and recording your responses so you can see how you look and perform when it's being recorded (you might notice an awkward habit that you do without noticing). Do this as many times as possible in combination with the previously mentioned preparation tips and you'll be on your way to successfully acing online interviews in no time.

TELEPHONE INTERVIEWS

Given the rise of the HireVue interview, telephone interviews aren't as popular as they once were. The typical route you'll go through with most firms is, after successfully completing a HireVue interview, you'll be invited in for an assessment centre or in-person interview(s). However, some firms do still use telephone interviews in their hiring process and so it's good to be aware of them.

Personally, I think telephone interviews are the most straightforward to get through since there's no screen that you need to constantly be looking at, there's no one directly in front of you that you need to be conscious of, you don't need to worry about how you look, and so on. To add to this, you can have all of your notes spread out in front of you to help you with any and every competency, behavioural, or technical question that gets thrown your way. All you need to do is make sure you prepare well beforehand and then the rest should be plain sailing.

In terms of the structure of telephone interviews, they're pretty much the same as the standard 30-minute interview where most of it will focus on competency and behavioural-style questions with the inclusion of a few technical questions, and possibly a brain teaser.

Lastly, you should try and figure out whether you prefer standing up and walking around whilst talking on the phone or whether you're more composed when sitting down to do your telephone interview. This might seem somewhat insignificant, but believe me it can have a huge impact on your interview performance. For example, I personally prefer taking calls whilst on a walk outside, or standing up and doing laps around the room I'm in. I feel this allows me to get the juices flowing as opposed to sitting at a desk staring at a screen or any notes in front of me that I don't immediately need. Find what works best for you and be sure to create an environment conducive to success.

IN-PERSON INTERVIEWS

Rather than focusing on the structure of these interviews, which is typically the same as all the other interviews mentioned earlier in this chapter, I want to use this section to focus on some of the things that many candidates completely disregard or are never told about preparing for, and why you should consider doing and being aware of these in order to maximise your chances of leaving your best impression on the interviewers and subsequently improving your chances of securing an offer. These include small talk to and from the interview room, why you should always take people up on their water offering, mastering your elevator pitch, reading the news on the morning of your interview, making eye contact and addressing everyone in the room, referring to people by their names, and preparing strong questions.

Small Talk

Rocking up to the front desk or reception area of an investment bank can be an unnerving experience, especially if it's your first time. It can also be quite exciting and inspiring knowing that you've been selected by this prestigious organisation to potentially work in these exact offices.

Typically, after you arrive and let the receptionist know that you've got an interview, they'll tell you to take a seat as they notify your interviewer that you've arrived. And then, a few minutes later (if you're not told to go directly to the interview room), the person interviewing you will come down, meet you (make sure you practise your firm handshake), and then take you up to the interview room.

The last thing you want to do between being taken from the reception area to the interview room is to be silent, awkward, and have nothing to talk about with your interviewer. This is where small talk comes in, and it is more important than you may think. The same applies after the interview when you might be walked from the interview room back to reception. So, what exactly is small talk and how do you prepare for it? Well, it's actually pretty simple and straightforward. Small talk is the polite, casual, often non-work-related and unimportant conversations people have over a brief interaction.

Whether it's the weather, a major event happening in the news, asking the person how their day is going, or something financial markets-related, be prepared with at least two to four questions you'd feel comfortable asking in order to avoid any awkward silences. Rest assured, most of the time they'll be asking you the questions, but it's good to have some questions of your own to ask them as a two-way conversation is almost always more interesting and engaging than a one-sided conversation.

Why does this all matter? Well, it matters for you because small talk nurtures likeability, and likeability plays a larger role in securing offers and succeeding in interviews than people think. For example, you can be the smartest person in the world, but if you're a pain to work with or you're outright rude to everyone you meet, chances are nobody will hire you or want to work with you.

I always tell students and graduates that the company you're interviewing with already knows you're smart and capable. That's what they've gathered from your application, CV, and cover letter, and essentially why you've been invited in for an interview. The interview is just a way for the team that's hiring to identify the most suitable candidate, and whether they're genuinely interested in the role and curious about the nature of the work (it's better to hire someone who actually wants to be there as opposed to hiring someone who's only interested in the pay package and prestige of the role).

Therefore, before your next interview be sure to create a list of questions that you'd feel comfortable asking during small talk with the interviewer in order to build rapport and avoid awkward moments and silences.

Take the Water

You'll very likely be offered a cup of water by the person interviewing you. Always accept the offer. First, it's not a big deal, it doesn't cause them to go out of their way, they won't offer it if they don't mean it, and it costs nothing other than a minute of their time. And second, having a cup of water can be a useful tool to help you pause or gain some time to think about the answer to a question if you're ever struggling.

This might sound bizarre, but oftentimes we simply need a way to gather ourselves. As such, if you don't have a cup of water in front of you and you face a difficult question or awkward moment in the interview you won't know how best to act and compose yourself, and instead you're more likely to say the first thing that comes to mind, which is often not the best answer.

In contrast, if you did have a cup of water in front of you, it's completely normal to take a sip, pause, and think about the answer you want to give—even if you're keeping the interviewer waiting for a few seconds. To add to that, and while we're on the topic of answer delivery, it's worth mentioning that it's much better to take a moment, with or without the water, and genuinely think for a few seconds before giving your answer to the interviewer. They'll actually prefer this as it shows you're a thoughtful candidate who actually takes the time to consider the questions that are asked in the interview as opposed to just another candidate who automatically sputters out a pre-rehearsed answer.

Master Your Elevator Pitch

Whether you're in an elevator or an interview, at some point in your journey to landing an offer you'll be asked 'Tell me about yourself', and there are two ways that you can approach this question.

The first way is if you're not in an interview and you know the person just wants a short answer. In which case your elevator pitch will focus on who you are, what you study and at which university, any titles or roles you hold as part of an extracurricular activity (if it's finance-related), your career interests, and if it makes sense you can tell them why you're there today (e.g. if it's a networking event or something else that isn't an interview).

The second way to pitch yourself is to focus on three things. Your background story, the pivotal moment that opened your eyes to the world of finance, and what you've done since then to broaden your knowledge and end up with an interview. By having this structure you're able to paint a picture in the interviewer's mind of your personal story, which in return will make them understand you better, potentially resonate with parts of your journey, but most of all they'll appreciate the bias for action and all the work you've put in to successfully get to where you are today. After all, everyone likes 'go-getters' and so you should give them an insight into the journey that brought you to where you are today.

The easiest way to master your elevator pitch is to say it in the mirror, and record and review your response at least 100 times. After you've done that, I'm pretty confident that you'll have a solid answer. If you need additional help, you can always reach out to your peers or those who have offers to review your pitch. Alternatively, you can feed an artificial intelligence tool like ChatGPT tons of information on who you are, your background, how you became interested in the world of finance, why you're interested in the particular division you're applying to, and so on, then ask it to help you tweak and improve your current elevator pitches. Be sure to have them reviewed, however, as artificial intelligence tools are far from perfect.

Read the News the Day of Your Interview

As an interviewer, the easiest way for me to find out if you, the candidate, genuinely stay up-to-date with current affairs and aren't just preparing for commercial awareness as a chore is for me to ask you if you saw what's going on in the financial markets this morning, and then pause and wait for your response. Markets are dynamic and always changing, and so what you read the other day, or the articles you've prepared to talk about should any commercial awareness questions be asked, can oftentimes already be outdated (that isn't to say you shouldn't use them). The point I'm trying to make is that this industry is always changing and so it requires individuals to keep abreast of what's going on in the markets on a daily basis.

Think of it like this, if you miss something big that happened in the markets in the morning (e.g. a huge interest rate change or a major investment bank defaulting) and this news heavily impacts your book of clients but you're unaware of it, it really won't look good. The last thing you want is for the client to call you for an update, but you don't have a clue what they're talking about.

Therefore, on the day of your interview you want to do two things from a commercial awareness perspective. First, keep an eye on the levels and prices of major indices (FTSE 100, S&P 500, NASDAQ, etc.), currency pairings (EUR/USD, USD/JPY, GBP/USD, etc.), and commodities (Gold, Oil, etc.). Second, you want to read any major news or events (particularly stories directly related to the role you're interviewing for) so you can be sure you don't get caught off guard.

It's the Small Things That Matter

When preparing for interviews a lot of candidates can find themselves obsessed over the major areas of interview preparation (technical questions, competency skills, etc.) and completely forget about basic manners and common courtesy when they're in the interview. As such, it's always important to remember that it's the small things that can often leave the largest impression on someone whom you've just interacted with. When I say 'the small things' I mean eye contact, addressing everyone in the room, referring to people's names, and actively listening.

Let's start with the first one, making and keeping *eye contact*. I used to struggle to make eye contact with people. It might have been an introvert or confidence thing, but it definitely didn't give off the best impression. When you're interviewing someone who struggles to make eye contact it can immediately signal a lack of interest, low confidence, low self-esteem, and a general lack of interpersonal skills, all of which are extremely important in roles in the world of finance and banking. After all, you'll be expected to work as part of a team, communicate effectively with colleagues, and potentially attend client meetings. So it's important to fix any eye contact issues before they get in the way of your career.

If you struggle to make eye contact with people, my advice is to practise as many in-person mock interviews as you can. With each one you should make a mental note of making eye contact so as to intentionally improve it. You can also make a conscious effort in your day-to-day interactions to try and hold eye contact with the people you interact with for a few seconds and gradually build up. Feel free to practise eye contact on video calls by looking at the person's eyes on screen, but keep in mind this isn't as good as practising eye contact in person.

The second method is to simply improve your confidence in the topics you talk about. If eye contact is often a confidence issue, it makes sense to tackle the route of the problem. And I've learnt from public speaking that my confidence when presenting in front of an audience is directly correlated to the level of knowledge I have about the topic I'm presenting on. So master what you're talking about and you'll naturally increase your confidence, and hopefully your ability to make eye contact.

Next up is all about making an intentional effort to *address everyone in the room*. Sometimes you might be interviewed by more than one person. In this case, you should make a conscious effort to share your responses to questions across the room (to all interviewers). The last thing you want is to come across as someone who only addresses the most senior person in the room, or the candidate who totally ignored the male/female in the room.

Third is to do with making a conscious effort to *refer to people using their names*. As human beings, our favourite word in the English language is our own name. Do this and people will naturally warm to you, appreciate the fact that you made an effort to remember their name, and respect your professional demeanour.

Last but not least, you need to display *active listening* skills. Actively listening is the ability to listen carefully to what someone has to say and then respond in a way that shows you understand. It's quite a broad term and also includes doing things like keeping eye contact, nodding when you understand something, asking follow-up questions because you didn't quite understand something that was being said, referring back to something that was said a few minutes ago, and so on. These are all ways in which you can show the interviewer that you're actually paying attention to what they're saying rather than ignoring them and instead just thinking about what you're going to say next.

Questions to Ask

At the end of every interview, you'll have the opportunity to ask a question or two. If you don't have any questions for the interviewer, it's safe to assume that you won't be put through to the next stage of the hiring process. Why? Well, not preparing any questions will give the impression that you don't really care about the role or opportunity, are not taking the hiring process seriously, and are less prepared than most of the other candidates. Instead, what you want to do is prepare at least two questions—one that's division or role-specific and another that's interviewer-specific.

The division or role-specific question tells the interviewer that you've thought about the division or role in detail, and it gives them an opportunity to teach you something. Although this type of question is expected, it's an easy win. Examples of such questions can include:

- *Investment banking.* Can you tell me about a recent deal the team worked on, and what challenges or opportunities you encountered during the process? What major trends do you see shaping the M&A (or capital markets) landscape over the next few years, and how is your team positioning itself to adapt?
- *Sales and trading.* How closely does the sales team work with traders, and how do they collaborate to deliver the best outcome for clients?
- *Asset management.* How do portfolio managers here balance short-term market movements with long-term investment strategies?

224

- *Equity research.* How do analysts in equity research balance covering a broad sector with providing in-depth analysis on individual companies, and how do you prioritise research efforts?
- *Private wealth management.* How does your team customise investment strategies for high-net-worth clients with diverse financial goals?
- *Technology.* What role does artificial intelligence and machine learning play in the firm's technology strategy, and how do you see these technologies evolving?
- *Operations.* What initiatives is the operations team currently working on to improve efficiency or streamline processes?
- *Human resources.* How does human resources contribute to maintaining and promoting the firm's culture, especially as the firm grows and hires new talent?
- *Compliance.* How does the compliance team collaborate with other departments, like legal and operations, to ensure seamless adherence to regulations?

The second type of question you want to ask is the interviewer-specific question. At the end of the day, we all love talking about ourselves. It feels good. And guess what, if you can make someone feel good about themselves, they're more likely to enjoy your company and lean towards putting you through to the next stage of the hiring process. Try to think of questions that you're genuinely curious about. Here are a few examples worth considering:

- What do you enjoy most about working at this firm, and separately the division, and what keeps you here?
- Can you share a little about your career path and how you got to your current role?
- What's been the most challenging project you've worked on during your time here?

- How would you describe the culture of the team you work with, and how does it compare to the overall firm culture?
- What skills or qualities do you believe are most important to succeed in this role and at this firm?
- How does the firm support your personal and professional growth, and what opportunities have you taken advantage of?
- How does the firm handle work–life balance, especially in busy periods?
- What's the one thing you wish you had known before starting your role here?
- What advice would you give someone in my shoes who's interested in breaking into this industry?
- What do you think differentiates employees who excel in their careers here from those who struggle?

These questions show genuine curiosity about the interviewer's experience while also giving you valuable insights into the firm's culture, expectations, and opportunities for growth and development. They also allow for a more conversational tone during the interview and should help you stand out as an engaged and thoughtful candidate.

FINAL-ROUND INTERVIEWS

If you've reached a partner or final-round interview, it's pretty safe to say that you've shown the organisation that you're bright, capable, and have relevant experience on your CV. But now, you need to convert that potential into an impressive interview performance.

The thing with final-round interviews is that they're very rarely like the standard competency, behavioural, or technical interviews you'd have done beforehand. They're typically an informal conversation between you and the managing director, partner, or some other senior person from the team that's hiring. These final-round interviews will feel more like a casual chat with the manager, who essentially wants to get a sense of who you are and whether they think you'll fit in with the team. They'll be trying to get to know you and want to understand your personality and background beyond what's on paper. The three main qualities they'll be looking for are genuine interest in the business, fit, and potential. Let's go through these one by one.

Genuine Interest

The senior professional interviewing you will want to see whether you have a real passion for the role and the team or division's work. As such, what you'll need to do is express a sense of genuine curiosity and intrigue about the work that's being done in the role. If you seem uninterested or disengaged, they'll have little reason to give you an offer since anyone without a real interest in the work is unlikely to perform or progress over the long term. Keep abreast of relevant industry trends and current events (these senior professionals will always want to hear your commercial views and will likely dig deeper into why you think something is a certain way), especially those related to the specific division you're applying to. Last but not least, genuine interest can't be faked. So the best tactic when it comes to applying to firms is to try and find a role or division that you're actually interested in.

The last thing you want to do is to 'fake' it. Don't act like you're genuinely interested in the role if you're not. It's not uncommon to be asked who the CEO of the company or division is, or what price the company's stock is currently trading at. These are basic questions you'd be expected to know the answers to, unless you really didn't care about the role, division, or company itself.

Fit

Arguably the most important factor in making a hiring decision is whether you'll be a good fit for the team you've applied to. Companies thrive when their employees work well together and align with the company culture. As such, the hiring manager will likely have checked with other interviewers about how well you might fit within the team. Whether you fit the culture of the firm matters because, without it, even a highly skilled individual might struggle to thrive in the firm. The best way for you to gauge a company's culture is by asking previous interviewers or others in the firm for their experiences and insight regarding the culture. Take notes and try to highlight some of these traits (name-drop where you can) in the final-round interview.

Potential

The final thing the interviewer wants to see is your potential to grow, develop, and increasingly contribute to the team, division, and firm over time. In the world of banking and finance, people hire with a long-term view. Yes, it's common for people to join and move on after two or so years. In this industry, companies want candidates who aren't only competent but also motivated, driven, and determined to progress and climb within the firm.

If you can demonstrate that you're enthusiastic, proactive, and ambitious you'll do well. Ideally, you want to show that you're willing to get your hands dirty, open to do the boring and mundane tasks, prepared to take on challenges, work hard, and eventually move up within the team. The best way to convey this is by sharing your long-term goals, preparing questions that give the impression that you're focused on your long-term career prospects, and showing ambition for positions you hope to grow into and achieve down the line.

Preparation Tips

If you can exhibit genuine interest, demonstrate cultural fit, and show potential for growth, you'll stand out in any final-round interview. At this stage it's really just their opportunity to get to know you a little better. A kind of final check from a partner or senior manager who has spent decades in the field. Be yourself and be as authentic as you can be, as they'll know if you're putting on a facade.

In terms of preparation, you should prepare for final rounds as you would any other interview. Know why you want to join the firm, why you want to join the division you're interviewing for, and why you're the ideal candidate for the role. And be sure to have your competency, behavioural, brain teaser, and technical interview answers ready just in case.

Additionally, you want to make sure you're staying up-to-date on key global and financial news stories. Don't just memorise articles, instead aim to have an opinion on them. This will help you have interesting conversations, which are important as a good commercial conversation can set you miles apart from all the other candidates. Why is this the case? Well, think of it from the managing director's or partner's perspective. They're in the business of making money, whether it be for their clients or for the firm. And a large part of doing so requires knowledge about what's important to clients and the business as a whole. As such, a commercially aware candidate is an attractive potential addition for the team. Not to mention, being commercially aware is effectively a competitive advantage as it shows that you understand the broader context of the business world, the industry, and the specific firm you're applying to.

Lastly, it's completely normal to be nervous ahead of a final-round interview. The firm sees something in you, otherwise you wouldn't have made it this far in the process. Now all you have to do is be yourself, over-prepare to build your confidence, enjoy the process, and before you know it, you'll be signing your offer contract.

CHAPTER 20

DECIDING ON A DIVISION

D eciding on a division is one of the most difficult things for students and graduates to do. Most students either apply for the most attractive and highest-paying roles, which also tend to be the most competitive, or they end up with a scattergun approach applying for any and every division that's receiving applications. A better approach to applications would be to think more strategically with regard to the divisions you consider applying to.

In this chapter, I'm going to talk you through some of the key areas and factors that you should think about before considering doubling down on breaking into a specific division or area within the industry. I'll touch on the following: skills and strengths, career goals and long-term growth, personality fit and work style, work–life balance, compensation and incentives, interest in market trends and industry news, learning and development opportunities, client focus versus technical focus, division culture and environment, and exit opportunities, transferable skills, and mobility.

SKILLS AND STRENGTHS

Breaking into banking requires taking a strategic and tactical approach in order to maximise your chances of success. As such, breaking into the industry is all about playing to your strengths. Why? Because it's highly competitive and extremely difficult to get a foot in the door, especially given the limited time frame within which you have to apply to firms, and although it's not impossible it is extremely difficult to try and master a bunch of new skills in such a short period of time. So it makes sense to focus on your existing key strengths and core skills.

What I suggest you do, and this is what I did when I was in your shoes, is to identify three to five of your most developed (or currently being developed) skills. For me, these were public speaking, presentation skills, and interpersonal skills (i.e. communication and listening, commercial awareness, and teamwork). These were the core areas that I felt most accomplished and strongest in. So at the time, if I was asked by an interviewer whether I had any of these skills, I would have found it extremely easy and straightforward to talk at length about how I had the given skill, using multiple examples from academia, work, and life experiences to talk about how I'd developed the skill, why I'd enjoyed developing it, and why I thought it was valuable and made me suitable for the role I was applying for (i.e. sales roles rather than technical roles).

Therefore, I'd recommend identifying your strongest three to five skills and strengths as they'll make life a lot easier when deciding on the roles or divisions that are most suitable for you. After all, each division and business within the world of banking and finance requires something different from its potential employees. For example, in sales and trading you're expected to be exceptional at working under pressure and have a high level of market knowledge, whilst in investment banking or equity research you're expected to know your way around Excel to create financial models (and having analytical skills is more likely to play a part as you'll be analysing the financial data of companies).

So focus on identifying your key skills and strengths, and figure out which division(s) and role(s) they're most suited to.

CAREER GOALS AND LONG-TERM GROWTH

Whenever you have some time, it's worth mapping out your long-term career goals. This can be quite a tricky exercise, especially early on in your career, but be bold and highly ambitious. Once done, try and see how each division aligns with your long-term career goals. For example, if you want to become a portfolio manager or work for a hedge fund making lots of money managing portfolios, then it would make sense to start off in areas such as asset management or trading. In contrast, if you know you'd like to be building a book of clients and helping bring in revenue to the business from a sales perspective, then it makes sense to consider sales roles in either asset management or private wealth management. Finally, if you know you want to eventually break into private equity then it might make sense to focus on breaking into the investment banking division first, build up your experience in mergers, acquisitions, capital raising, and so on, and then prepare yourself for a move at the right time.

Research typical career paths within each division and identify if they're aligned with your own expectations around career growth and development.

PERSONALITY FIT AND WORK STYLE

Figure out whether you're the type of person who would prefer to be sat at a desk all day concentrating and focusing on doing intense, deep work, or if you'd much rather have a day that's got a variety of meetings, client interactions and pitches, networking, work-related social events, and so on. Assessing your own working style and preferences is an important factor in identifying a career path that's suitable for you. The last thing you want is to enter a division or role where the expectations of the work day and environment are the complete opposite of your own expectations.

WORK–LIFE BALANCE

You need to be realistic about the hours you're willing to work, especially early on in your career when you'll have the most energy. Working in the world of finance and banking isn't your typical nine to five and so you can expect to earn more than the typical nine to five. However, there are differences in working hours across divisions. The most notable difference is that between the front and back office. If you're not willing to work for 12–18 hours every weekday, and sometimes on weekends, for the first few years of your career then the front office might not be the right fit for you. Alternatively, it might make more sense to focus on applying to roles within the back office where the typical hours are a lot shorter (9–12 hours a day) than those expected in the front office.

COMPENSATION AND INCENTIVES

Compensation packages and expectations will differ from division to division, firm to firm, seniority level to seniority level, and role to role. At the early stages of your professional career all you need to really know is that the front office compensates its employees more handsomely (in terms of base salaries and bonuses) compared to the back office. However, the higher pay will come at the cost of more pressurised working environments, higher expectations, longer working hours, poorer work–life balance, and more. Therefore, it's worth figuring out whether you're willing to work harder to earn more, or if you're happy earning less by not working in one of the more 'popular' divisions within the industry that likely has better exit opportunities and room for growth and development.

INTEREST IN MARKET TRENDS AND INDUSTRY NEWS

Are you someone who thoroughly enjoys keeping up-to-date with world news and what's been going on in the financial markets? I'm talking to those of you who are naturally interested in economics and the pulse of the financial markets. If this is you, then areas such as sales and trading, asset management, equity research, and investment banking would be suitable areas worth considering a career in.

If, on the other hand, the thought of financial markets and news stories related to the world of finance are a bore to you, then your efforts to break into the industry might be better aimed at a division that doesn't require you to religiously stay up-to-date. These divisions could include operations, technology, finance, human resources, and so on.

LEARNING AND DEVELOPMENT OPPORTUNITIES

One piece of advice I like to give students and graduates is to focus on careers not where they'll earn the most, but where they'll learn the most.

In the first decade of your career it's better to focus on career opportunities that provide unique and steep learning curves because being able to learn and develop as much as possible, and as often as possible, will enable you to unlock new opportunities, see the world differently, and think in a way that continues to enable you to grow and develop. This will benefit you over the long term and naturally unlock higher-paying opportunities as time goes on. The alternative is to enter roles where the learning curve is flat and your work feels mundane, repetitive, and boring. In this case, even if the pay is great, your development and career opportunities are stagnant and will likely lead to limited long-term career growth.

CLIENT FOCUS VERSUS TECHNICAL FOCUS

Ask yourself whether you prefer client-focused work (sales, client relationship management, investor relations, private banking, etc.) or technical-focused work (technology, quantitative research, trading, building financial models, etc.). Client-centric careers require individuals who find relationship-building, socialising, networking, presenting, and communicating easy to do, whilst technical-centric careers require less of the soft skills that a client-focused role might benefit from, but a high level of hard skills such as technical acumen, problem-solving capabilities, attention to detail, and so on.

Understanding which type of career is more suitable for you based on your existing skills is extremely important when it comes to applications and interviews. For example, having the self-awareness to apply for the roles that make sense for you will result in being interviewed by people in these roles. As a result, you're more likely to connect with them and build rapport because you're both likely to share similar interests and skills.

DIVISION CULTURE AND WORKING ENVIRONMENT

You might not be aware of this, but within the same bulge bracket investment bank, you can expect to see different cultures across the different divisions. For example, the working environment within the investment banking division is typically one that might reflect a quiet day (and night) studying in the university library ahead of a big exam. Everyone's dialled in and focused, concentrating on building or reviewing financial models or client presentations. In contrast, the working environment on the trading floor is the complete opposite. You've got people shouting across the room to each other, tons of phones constantly ringing, lots of background noise, conversations and interactions going on, which you might either love to work with or hate because it makes concentrating extremely difficult.

In addition, the culture across divisions can be quite different too. For example, since the trading floor is quite individualistic, fast-paced, pressurised, intense, and cutthroat, it makes sense for it to be an environment with a competitive culture. Whereas in asset management or operations, the working environment is less pressurised and fast-paced, and conducive to a more collaborative and team-oriented working culture.

EXIT OPPORTUNITIES, TRANSFERABLE SKILLS, AND MOBILITY

Spending time in any career will equip you with a different toolkit of personal and professional skills. Banking and finance careers are no different. Spending time in the investment banking division would create a different version of you versus if you spent time in asset management, on the trading floor, or in the campus recruitment team within human resources. This is why it's worth thinking about the potential exit opportunities, transferable skills, and mobility you can expect to unlock and develop after spending a few years in the roles you hope to break into.

First, you want to look back on your long-term career goals and identify whether the roles you're considering applying to will increase the likelihood of securing your desired role(s) later on. Typically, front-office roles tend to have the best exit opportunities across the world of finance and outside of the industry too. This is because they're often seen as training grounds where junior professionals embark on extremely steep learning curves and develop highly sought-after skills (both soft and hard) for a range of industries.

Second, you want to assess the transferable skills you'll master having spent a few years in a given role, and whether these will be useful for the roles and career opportunities you want to pursue in the next three to five years.

Third, you want to keep in mind potential mobility opportunities. Let's say you want to eventually work in a front-office division but are struggling to secure any offers at present. In this case (mind you, a very common case), it would make sense to try and break into the operations or risk management divisions since they work closely with the front-office divisions. The key thing here is that you're focusing on opportunities where the mobility potential makes sense. For example, there's a clear pathway to move from operations or risk management into the front office if you're able to prove yourself with solid performance and consistently rank in the top quartile for your end-of-year reviews. People are always leaving the front office for opportunities elsewhere, and seats naturally open up for you to apply to. Internal mobility is a big part of hiring for almost every bulge bracket investment bank, and so positioning yourself accordingly and having the patience and maturity to take a long-term view can work wonders.

Taking into consideration all of the above will give you a clearer understanding of which division(s) best align with your personal and professional ambitions. Try to balance your interests, strengths, and lifestyle preferences in order to find the perfect division for you to break into and thrive in.

CHAPTER 21

LINKEDIN AND NETWORKING

Linkedln is an extremely powerful platform and tool for anyone serious about building their career. Used in the right way it can unlock both commercial and personal career opportunities. In this chapter, I'll focus on sharing advice and best practices on how you can get the most out of the platform as someone focused on breaking into the industry.

But first, here's a little background on why I'm a LinkedIn advocate. Before joining Goldman Sachs full-time, I was always interested in and understood the power of building a personal brand on the internet. I enjoyed the idea of digital leverage, such as being able to post something online and have someone on the other side of the world read and take something from it. I then thought it would be a good idea to start sharing my successes, public-speaking engagements, and general advice and interests on LinkedIn. And so that's what I did. This allowed me to have a positive impact all over the world without leaving the comfort of my chair. Over time, my profile grew, and if I'm being honest, it felt amazing.

However, things really started taking off when I joined Goldman Sachs. I can't lie, being associated with such a prestigious brand was powerful and came with many of its own perks. As a side note, this is something worth thinking about when deciding between two job offers. Which company has the more powerful or 'well-known' brand name attached to it? It might sound insignificant or a non-issue, but trust me, it can be the difference between unlocking or missing out on future opportunities. Having 'Analyst, Goldman Sachs' as my title on LinkedIn was a major unfair advantage, especially given my unconventional story of coming from a less-advantaged background, failing my first year of A-levels, and not attending an elite target university. But there I was, posting once (sometimes twice) a week, receiving tons of appreciation for the posts as well as thousands of connection requests, connecting with tons of people (students and industry professionals across seniority levels), and racking followers.

Over the last few years, I've used LinkedIn to share career advice, insights that I've personally found interesting and worth sharing, and tips for students and young professionals who are interested in breaking into the world of banking and finance. As a result, I've maxed-out my connections at 30,000, have grown a following of 60,000 professionals, and have been awarded the 'Top Voice' title. I don't share this information to toot my own horn. In fact, having so many connections and followers proves extremely useful. It's an asset that I value highly and put to use often. For example, I'm only one message away from 30,000 professionals working in the industry that I can reach out to any time a mentee or student of mine needs to be put in touch with someone in a given firm, division, and seniority level.

This level of access is extremely valuable and valued. But you don't need this many connections or followers in order to maximise your chances of connecting with industry professionals on LinkedIn. All you need is a tried and tested, tactical and mentor-first approach. And that's what I'll teach you to do in the next few pages.

THE POWER OF WEAK TIES

An important concept worth making a mental note of is 'the power of weak ties'. This addresses the misconception that the greatest career opportunities will mostly arise from our immediate and closest relationships. Research shows that job leads and valuable introductions often come from acquaintances rather than close friends. As such, by growing your network on LinkedIn, you're creating those valuable weak ties that can lead to unexpected opportunities if nurtured properly.

HOW TO APPROACH NETWORKING

As a first step, before reaching out to anyone, you need to make sure you're setting yourself up for success, not failure. The way to do this is to create and complete your LinkedIn profile as best as you can, sharing as much expected and relevant information as is reasonable. Optimising your profile in this way will send a message to anyone you reach out to and tell them who you are, what your career goals and ambitions are, and the extent of your skillset. Once you've done this, added a nice headshot, relevant background or cover image, and filled in your experiences, you're ready to start connecting with people.

Start connecting with people you know, like family, friends, teachers, lecturers, and alumni from your school. Don't be shy about reaching out to professionals in industries that interest you. These individuals will likely receive tons of connection requests, so they're highly unlikely to remember anyone they reject. Don't take it personally if you get rejected. In fact, you should expect to get rejected a whole lot more than you get accepted. And I get it, some of you might be wondering if it's weird to reach out to people you don't know. In all honesty, it probably is a little weird. But guess what, LinkedIn was built for networking. Every individual can benefit from building their own network. As such, don't just go around thinking that students and graduates are the main beneficiaries of connecting with industry professionals. That's not entirely true. Industry professionals are just as keen on connecting with the future leaders, experts, and industry professionals (i.e. you) as they are on connecting with established professionals.

Most people on LinkedIn aren't LIONs (LinkedIn Open Networkers). But the way to find the LIONs is by trial and error via connecting with as many relevant and interesting people as you can. It might seem daunting, particularly for the introverts out there, but my advice to you is not to overthink any of this. More importantly, have a bias for action, understand that this will increase your chances of landing your dream role in the world of finance and banking, and just execute on the task at hand.

The good thing is that once you start making connections, LinkedIn's algorithm will get to work and recommend additional people based on these connections, which can help grow your network even more.

LEVERAGING RECRUITERS

Most students and graduates seem to be unaware of the fact that LinkedIn is a hunting ground for specialist recruiters and recruitment firms interested in placing candidates in high-paying positions. Every time a candidate is successfully placed in a role, the recruiter takes a commission or generates revenue in some way, shape, or form. Their incentives and interests are aligned with yours if you're looking to break into the industry. As such, this is another reason why your profile should be optimised and perfected—you never know who'll come across it. Connect with finance recruitment firms and recruiters operating in the space so that you're on their radar (even if you're not interested in new opportunities). They'll often surprise you with the opportunities that they can offer in terms of titles, salaries, and so on.

HOW TO REACH OUT TO INDUSTRY PROFESSIONALS

The easiest way to get ahead of the competition when it comes to networking on LinkedIn is by actually reaching out to people and being strategic in your approach. Most students' and graduates' approach to cold outreach is the opposite of what it should be. They type paragraphs and essays of text, ask for ten different favours, totally disregard the reader's time and schedule, and often write with an air of entitlement. Doing any of these is a surefire way to getting ignored or even blocked.

The Message

What you want to do is the opposite of everything above. Keep your message short and easy to read or skim over, have one ask and one ask only, be conscious of the reader's busy work life and schedule, show them that you respect their time by offering to be flexible and work around what works best for them, be humble and let them know you totally understand if they're too busy, but you appreciate them taking the time to read your message. It's the small things that make the biggest difference. After all, these individuals are just humans like you and me. If you're respectful towards them, they'll feel more inclined to respond and help you out. When you're reaching out to people, you should constantly be thinking of ways to make the 'yes' as easy as possible (i.e. focus on how you can make it easier for them to say 'yes' to giving you some of their precious time, rather than ignore or reject your message).

Seek Mutual Affiliations

Another simple way to increase your response rate from reaching out to people on LinkedIn is to focus on messaging people whom you have some sort of mutual affiliation with. This could be the fact that they're an alumni of your university or specific course, or that you went to the same school or college, or you both attend the same club outside of work and academia, so on and so forth. Whatever it is, by mentioning the mutual affiliation in your message or subject line, it'll naturally make them more feel more inclined (and so be more likely) to respond to you.

Follow, Like, and Comment

If you want to play the long game, you should identify someone you'd like to connect with at some point down the line, but start nurturing the relationship now, before you actually reach out to them. This is where the follow–like–comment strategy comes into play. As the name suggests, follow them, go to their profile and explore their most recent posts, if any, and where relevant (without being weird) leave a comment, ideally on posts where they're adding value to the reader (as opposed to a personal post, which would be quite weird for you, a complete stranger, to comment on). I admit, this strategy is tricky to execute for finance professionals since you need to find someone who actually posts often, and most people in the world of finance tend to avoid posting on LinkedIn at all. However, if you do manage to find someone who's posting often and trying to share value with their audience, they'll appreciate your thoughtful comment(s) or questions on their posts, and over time they'll get to know you better, which will eventually provide a perfect time for you to message them privately. Try not to ask too much, too soon. Rather, be curious, make the interaction with them, and learn about their work. This will naturally make them want to help you out when the right time arises. The reason it's important to go on their profile and interact with more than one of their posts is so that LinkedIn knows you're interested in what they have to say. Once it knows this, whenever they post something going forward, it'll appear at the top of your feed when you open LinkedIn.

Focus on Alumni

When reaching out to people on LinkedIn you want to do everything you can to increase your chances of getting a response. As such, you should try and find the people in the roles, divisions, firms, or industries you're interested in who are alumni of your school or university. This goes back to identifying people with mutual affiliations to you. The more you do this, the more likely you are to actually hear back from them.

Focus on Junior Professionals

This is an important point most students and graduates completely disregard. You'll learn the most from people who are only a few steps ahead of you, not the industry veterans who have decades of experience. Therefore, you should prioritise reaching out to people with up to five years of experience more than you. For most students and graduates, this means messaging interns, analysts, and associates.

The reason why focusing on these individuals is important is because junior professionals would have been in your exact position not long ago. As such, how to break into the industry, how to prepare for interviews, how to go about learning about the division, and so on will be fresh in their minds ready to be shared with you. They know what the firms are looking for, they're carrying out a lot of the interviews, they're reviewing a lot of the CVs/résumés and cover letters that are submitted with applications. Compare this type of connection and insight with a catch-up with a managing director who was in university a few decades ago and can only offer you wisdom, as opposed to practical advice on breaking in. The former will be more useful for getting your foot in the door.

I'm not saying don't reach out to more senior professionals. By all means do reach out to them. Just be aware they might not respond as often and won't offer as immediate and practical advice as the junior professionals. However, they're good connections to have nonetheless, given their extensive industry experience, wisdom, and the potential for them to unlock opportunities for you, whether it be connecting you with people within their own network, or putting in a good word for you with HR.

Example Message

Having taken all of the above into consideration, here's a draft message you can use when reaching out to people on LinkedIn:

> Hi [their name], I hope you don't mind me reaching out to you. I'm [your name], a [current situation]. I noticed you [insert mutual affiliation] and thought I'd reach out. I'm interested in [career/industry] and would be immensely grateful for 15 minutes of your time to discuss [enter topic of interest or challenge you're currently facing and need help with]. I can be extremely flexible and work around your busy schedule. Having said this, I understand you must have many competing priorities, so if this isn't possible, please feel free to ignore or decline. Either way, thank you for your time. Best, [your name].

For more template messages and LinkedIn and email outreach resources visit www.afzalhussein.com.

Keep it short and polite, and make it easy for them to reply. Your message should be so good it makes them feel guilty to ignore or reject you, and instead makes them want to respond, help, or mentor you.

An important point worth mentioning is the sentence where you talk about the industry or career you're interested in. The more related this is to the professional's role, the better. By being specific about your interests in a career in the role they're actually working in, you make the request hyper-relevant and specific to them. This increases the likelihood that they'll reply and help you out, as they'll feel extremely qualified to do so. After all, they're an expert in the area you're most interested in. However, a word of warning. If you do this, make sure you're actually interested in the role or area as you can easily be found out for faking it, and nobody appreciates their time being wasted—especially if they're doing you a favour. Whatever you do, just make sure you prepare for the catch-up with them as if you're preparing for an interview.

When I tell students and graduates 'You can't just ask and take, you need to bring value to the person first' they get confused and wonder how on earth can they, a student or graduate, be of use to an industry professional. Well, the answer is simple. Bringing value to the table, or making an interaction or meeting worth someone's time, can be done in numerous ways. Think outside the box for a minute and see if you can think of a way to do so.

One way is to simply attend the meeting extremely prepared. By being prepared, you're bringing value. You're showing the person that you're taking this seriously and are not interested in taking advantage of or wasting their time. This shows your dedication and commitment to breaking into the industry and being a potential high-value mentee. Someone that will listen, get things done, and eventually succeed. This adds value to the meeting as it makes it worthwhile and productive for both parties. It'll also go a long way in building rapport and a strong connection with the professional. It's these subtle, small acts and gestures that people truly care about and appreciate.

And doing them often, and well, can be the difference between having deep connections with a broad range of industry professionals, or not.

When someone suggests 'grabbing a coffee', it doesn't have to mean literally getting coffee. It's just an informal, 30-minute conversation in a relaxed setting. Use this time to be yourself while staying professional—they're gauging your personality, curiosity, and how serious you are about your career. Be prepared. Go in with specific questions. Ask about their career, the pros and cons of their role, and any advice they'd give to someone in your position. But remember, it's not all about you—listen actively and look for ways you can add value, even if it's just showing genuine interest and appreciation for their time.

After the chat, don't let the relationship go cold. A simple follow-up message to thank them is crucial. Then, keep them updated on your progress occasionally—whether it's completing exams, landing interviews, or exploring new opportunities. These little check-ins keep the connection alive, and over time, these relationships can lead to referrals or introductions.

Bringing it all together, here are the steps to make LinkedIn work for you. Create a profile that represents you well. Connect broadly, including people you don't know personally but share your career interests. Engage with recruiters in your field. Send short, focused messages to potential contacts. Schedule coffee chats to build real connections. Follow up and keep these relationships alive. The key to LinkedIn networking is to keep building connections and maintaining them over time. Don't be that person who only reaches out when they need something. Create a habit of engaging with your network, sharing useful insights, and keeping people updated on your journey. By doing this, you'll set yourself apart and open doors that would have stayed closed otherwise.

CHAPTER 22

TACKLING IMPOSTER SYNDROME

Imposter syndrome is real. Especially if, like me, you come from a world where nobody you grew up around (friends, family, or relatives) worked or works in the industry you aspire to break into. Whether it's interviews, assessment centres, online applications, online tests, or doing the actual job and building a career in the world of banking and finance, it's quite frankly very common to feel like a fish out of water. It's completely normal to feel a sense of imposter syndrome, and that you somehow pulled one over on everyone and snuck into a place where you don't actually belong or qualify to be doing the role you've secured. And don't get me started on not going to an elite, target university, the industry jargon everyone so casually throws around, or the unspoken rules and etiquette in the industry that you didn't even know were a thing.

Either way, let me be the first to tell you that you're exactly where you need to be. Trust me. I used to think I was an imposter early on in my career until I realised and remembered that I broke into the industry on my own merit. Similarly, if you break into the industry, it's down to you earning your place on your spring week, your internship, or your full-time role. The industry professionals who said yes to your CV, cover letter, and performance in the assessment centres and interviews simply saw potential in you and agreed that there was a place in the industry for you.

As with many things, our imaginations tend to make us think that things are worse than they actually are, or that everyone around us is more knowledgeable about work and the industry than us, and that everyone other than us has it all figured out. This couldn't be further from the truth. You're not the only person walking around with these thoughts floating around in your head. Everyone else is still figuring 'it' out too. If they weren't figuring it out, they wouldn't be working so hard, limiting their lives to less than 30 days of annual leave each year, and instead would probably be travelling the world, doing something they're more interested in, spending more time with family and friends, or enjoying some form of early retirement. Trust me, nobody has it all figured out. So the next time you feel like an imposter, just know that you're exactly where you need to be.

CONCLUSION

The world of banking and finance employs individuals from all walks of life, creeds, and cultures. However, it's worth knowing that cultures can differ between organisations, and across divisions within organisations, and there's no way of knowing whether you'll 'fit in' or succeed in a particular role or company from the outset. The only way to find out is to throw yourself in at the deep end and explore career opportunities until you find something that feels like a good fit. This can take a year for some, 20 years for others, and forever for many. It'll differ for everyone. However, if you give up and settle, you'll never know what could have been. And one of the worst feelings ever is that of regret, so optimise for regret minimisation.

If there's one thing you take from this book, let it be this. The interviews, spring weeks, internships, graduate schemes, and full-time roles you manage to secure can pave the way for you to have a tremendous career spanning decades, if that's what you're truly after. Having said this, these experiences need not define your career trajectory and journey if you don't want them to. Only a handful of students and graduates immediately secure their dream roles at their dream company. I was fortunate enough to be one of them. But you should know that careers can be 40–50 years long. And if you don't want the first 5–10 years to determine the future trajectory of your career, it really doesn't have to.

Use these years to explore and learn about different companies, divisions, and industries, and get a feel for what you're extremely interested in because this is likely what you'll be extremely good at, and thus naturally excel in. Pay attention to what you read outside of the worlds of academia and work and use this insight to guide you. Because once you figure out what genuinely interests you, it's only a matter of time until you break into a relevant role.

Stay ambitious, maintain your drive, work extremely hard, have a bias for action, be consistent with your good habits, persevere through the tough times, and always pay it forward.

If you do this, I think you'll achieve more than you might expect.

Good luck. You got this!

INDEX